THE AGE OF THE ENLIGHTENMENT

Frederick The Great

International University Consortium
The University of Maryland University College
University Boulevard at Adelphi Road
College Park, Maryland 20742-1612
(301) 985-7811

961

7-2-90

The Open University
Arts: A Second Level Course
The Enlightenment

Units 15–16
Frederick the Great
Letters and Documents

Prepared for the Course Team by Tony Lentin

Daniel Chodowiecki, *Frederick the Great on Parade*, 1777, engraving. Dresden, Deutsche Fotothek.

The Open University Press

The Open University Press
Walton Hall, Milton Keynes
MK7 6AA

First published 1979. Reprinted 1983.

Designed by the Graphic Design Group of the Open University.

Typeset by Santype International Ltd, Salisbury, Wilts, and printed in Great Britain by
Waterlow Ltd, Dunstable, Member of BPCC plc.

ISBN 0 335 07608 4

This text forms part of an Open University course. The complete list of units in the course
appears at the end of this text.

For general availability of supporting material referred to in this text, please write to Open
University Educational Enterprises Limited, 12 Cofferidge Close, Stony Stratford, Milton
Keynes, MK11 1BY, Great Britain.

Further information on Open University courses may be obtained from the Admissions
Office, The Open University, P.O. Box 48, Walton Hall, Milton Keynes, MK7 6AB.

Contents

Study material

The letters and documents in Units 15–16 are described more fully on pp. 6–8.
In addition to the units, you might need to refer to the Course Anthology, '*The Age of Enlightenment*': *An Anthology of Eighteenth-Century Texts* Vol 1, edited by Simon Eliot and Beverley Stern (1979), Ward Lock Educational.

The broadcasts are an integral part of this block; they are:
Television programme 7   'Dinner at Baron D'Holbach's', a dramatization in which Frederick appears as intellectual and wit, the correspondent of the French *philosophes*
Television programme 8   'Frederick and Voltaire', a dramatization of Voltaire's visit to Frederick's court at Sans-Souci (1750–3)
Radio programme 15   'A Model of Despotism', a portrait of Frederick at Sans-Souci as seen by himself and his contemporaries
Radio programme 16   'War and Peace in the Age of Reason', a talk on international relations in Frederick's Europe, by M. S. Anderson, Professor of International History at the London School of Economics

Acknowledgements

My thanks are due to M. S. Anderson, Pauline Batchelor, Stuart Brown, Angus Calder, Stephanie Clennell, P. N. Furbank, Werner Futerman, David Goodman, Magnus John, Paul Kafno, Graham Martin and Keith Whitlock, and also to Irene Hatt, Pam McLaren and Raymond Munns; finally to the late Herman Simons for his critical admiration of Frederick the Great.

Aims

'If this ruler is not worthy of being King, I do not know who is.'

    d'Alembert (1763)

'The King of Prussia is confessedly the greatest King now in Europe.'

    James Boswell (1763)

From Units 10–12, on *The Decline and Fall of the Roman Empire*, you will remember how important fame and glory were to Gibbon. From Unit 3 on Epistle IV of Alexander Pope's *An Essay on Man*, you may also remember, as Nick Furbank put it, 'how central an issue "Greatness"—great houses, great funeral monuments, the leaving of a "great" name—was to the eighteenth century'. While other units deal with great books, great art or great music, Units 15–16 bring us face to face with someone whom everyone, even his enemies, recognized as a 'great man', though some also thought him one of the most wicked and unscrupulous who ever lived.[1] During the next fortnight you are asked to turn your attention to two units, two radio and two television programmes about Frederick the Great of Prussia (1712–86).

The units are based on letters and other documents by or concerning Frederick and comprise, to the best of my knowledge, the fullest selection of his writings now available in English. The eminent French literary critic, Lanson, has no hesitation in calling Frederick 'a great writer'. I would not myself claim for him the classic qualities of authors like Fielding, Hume, Gibbon or Voltaire. Even so, I hope you will find his works interesting in their own right. His letters in particular seem to me, as Lanson says, 'among the most interesting things to read that the eighteenth century has to offer'; interesting, because they illustrate the outlook of a ruler regarded by many of his contemporaries (to quote the historian M. S. Anderson) as 'the symbol of the Enlightenment enthroned'.

Most of the documents in this collection are by Frederick himself and present his views and his version of events. Where possible, I have also included in the commentary eyewitness accounts by contemporary foreign visitors to Prussia in the 1770s (such as Dr Moore and Dr Burney from Britain, the Comte de Guibert from France and Freiherr von Reisbeck from Germany) so that you have some evidence against which to test Frederick's self-presentation (which I happen to find unusually truthful and free from self-deception). Likewise, you can match Frederick's self-created image with the views of his contemporaries in the radio and television programmes, which are intended as an integral part of the block.

Frederick the Great ruled from 1740 to 1786. He directed Prussia's rise from a poor and unpretentious north German kingdom to a serious contender for political influence over Germany as a whole, with the status of a European Great Power. This he achieved in the course of two major wars, the War of the Austrian Succession (1740–8) and the Seven Years War (1756–63), in which he astounded Europe as an outstanding military commander. In the period after the Seven Years War his presence continued to dominate Europe, rather as Louis XIV's had done in the late seventeenth and early eighteenth century. But the prestige which Frederick commanded was not only on account of his victories, splendid and important though they were: Frederick was also uniquely interesting in being an active participant in the cultural and intellectual life of the Enlightenment. He was

---

[1] His lifelong enemy, Empress Maria Theresa of Austria, called him 'that wicked man'. George II of England, his uncle and ally, called him 'a malevolent rogue, a bad friend, bad ally, bad relation, bad neighbour— in short, the most dangerous trouble-maker in Europe'.

Figure 1 J. H. C. Franke, *Frederick the Great*, 1764, oil on canvas; photograph from Cambridge University Library. 'Toujours en vedette' ('Always on the alert'), Frederick the Great.

'I saw the King. It was a glorious sight. He was dressed in a suit of plain blue, with a star and a plain hat with a white feather. He had in his hand a cane. The sun shone bright. He stood before his palace, with an air of iron confidence that could not be opposed . . . I beheld the King who has astonished Europe by his warlike deeds. I beheld (pleasant conceit!) the great defender of the Protestant cause, who was prayed for in all the Scots kirks. I beheld the '*Philosophe de Sans-Souci*'' (James Boswell at Sans-Souci, 12 July 1764).

'He talked to me about literature, philosophy, even politics and war and peace. I would need a whole volume to give you an idea of his conversation. All I can tell you . . . is that the King impressed me as greater even than he is by reputation. He speaks of this reputation and of his glory with a modesty and calmness altogether worthy of him' (d'Alembert to Mlle de Lespinasse, 13 June 1763).

a poet, a musician, a flautist, a composer, an art connoisseur, an indefatigable conversationalist and man of letters, who wrote on history, politics, religion and literature, and was the close correspondent of Voltaire and d'Alembert,[2] each of whom visited him at Sans-Souci. He was a devotee of French culture, who affected to speak German 'like a coachman', and wrote his most important works in French. One nineteenth-century historian (C. Paganel) even claimed that 'he shared with Voltaire the intellectual supremacy of the eighteenth century'; and while you should judge for yourself whether this is not something of an exaggeration, it is significant that Frederick himself professed to be a 'philosopher by inclination, a

2 Contrast George II of England on Hogarth—'I hate painters and poets'; and George III—'still scribble, scribble, eh, Mr Gibbon?'; or even Joseph II of Austria—'Too many notes, Herr Mozart'.

politician out of duty'. 'The *philosophes*', d'Alembert informed him in 1770, 'and men of letters of every nation, have long regarded you, Sire, as their leader and their model.' It was this enigmatic combination of statesman and intellectual, warmonger and wit, in Frederick's character and career that exercised such an enduring fascination and earned him the reputation of a 'philosopher-prince' and an 'enlightened despot'.

In a sense, then, you can regard the 'text' in these units and the accompanying broadcasts as being the phenomenon and the personality of Frederick himself—'the incomparable Frederick', as Gibbon called him. The aims of the units and broadcasts are:

1   to introduce you to Frederick as he appeared to the world and as revealed by his thoughts on kingship, society and the state, law, religion, the arts, international relations, war and the Enlightenment;
2   to enable you to judge for yourself how far and in what sense (if at all) he deserves his reputation for 'greatness', and whether his own 'enlightenment' was genuine, or merely, as Professor Anderson and many other historians hold, 'a pretentious facade, covering policies which were selfish and even frivolous'.

Unless otherwise indicated, the translations of the documents are my own.

'Germany' in the eighteenth century

Figure 2   Germany in the eighteenth century

'Germany is undoubtedly a very fine country', wrote David Hume in 1748, 'full of industrious honest people: and were it united, it would be the greatest power that ever was in the world.' In the eighteenth century, however, 'Germany' was hardly more than a geographical expression. Far from being united, a single national state like Britain or France, Germany was a fragmented conglomeration of sovereign states. Numbering some 350 in all, they ranged from large electorates, like Hanover in the north or Bavaria in the south, to so-called Free Cities, like Frankfurt or Nuremberg; to tiny ecclesiastical principalities, like the electorates of Mainz or Cologne, and to independent territories only a few acres in size.

Nominally, all these states owed allegiance to the so-called 'Holy Roman Emperor' of Germany, a title established by Charlemagne in the ninth century, and since 1437 invariably conferred by the nine 'electors'[3] on the male head of the Austrian house of Habsburg.[4] By the eighteenth century, however, the Holy Roman Empire was, as Voltaire quipped, 'neither holy, nor Roman nor an empire', but a somewhat sentimental and toothless anachronism, to which much pious lip-service was paid. This barely screened the underlying complex mosaic of independent states, with clashing political, economic and even religious interests: Protestant in the north, Catholic in the south, often mutual rivals, often under foreign influence, and pawns on the chessboard of European diplomacy. The Elector of Bavaria, for example, traditionally aligned himself with France against Austria; Frederick the Great's uncle, George II of England, who was also Elector of Hanover, sided with Austria against Prussia in the 1740s, and with Prussia against Austria in the 1750s. Until the very end of the century there was little 'national' feeling in Germany: 'The Fatherland' invariably meant one's own particular state.

The rise of Brandenburg-Prussia

Brandenburg-Prussia was a relative upstart in Germany. It consisted of separate chunks of territory dispersed right across the North German plain: on the Rhine, Cleves and the Mark; on the Weser, Minden and Ravensburg; on the Elbe and on the Oder, Magdeburg, Halberstadt and the traditional heartland of Brandenburg; and East Prussia, which actually lay outside the Holy Roman Empire, cut off from Brandenburg by a wedge of Polish territory. The Elector of Brandenburg received the formal title of 'king' only in 1701, eleven years before Frederick's birth, and even in the mid-century Louis XV of France referred to Frederick not as King of Prussia, but, condescendingly, as 'the Marquis of Brandenburg', a provincial German princeling. Voltaire, more aptly, called him 'king of the border-strips' ('*roi des lisières*'), alluding to Prussia's long straggling frontier-lines, quite unprotected by natural geographical boundaries.

A succession of outstanding rulers forged this random chain of scattered territories into a powerful united state. The Hohenzollerns, electors of Brandenburg since the fifteenth century, became rulers of Prussia in 1618. Under the feeble rule of elector George William (1618–40), Prussia, though neutral, was devastated in the Thirty Years War. His son, Frederick-William, 'the Great Elector' (1640–88), was the founder of modern Prussia, building up a large army and smashing the independent powers of the nobility in his various lands in order to bring them under his own control. His son, Elector Frederick III (1688–1713), who proclaimed himself 'King in Prussia' in 1701, was, however, mainly devoted to aping the magnificent court of Louis XIV of France and, in so doing, he squandered Prussia's finances. His wife, the cultivated Sophia Charlotte, sister of George I of England, patronized the philosopher Leibniz.

---

[3] of Brandenburg, Hanover, Bavaria, Cologne, Mainz, Trier, Saxony, the Palatinate, Bohemia.

[4] The Habsburgs ruled over their own polyglot dominions, most of them outside Germany. In 1740 these included Austria, Hungary, Bohemia, Silesia and Belgium—in aggregate five times the size of Prussia.

Their son, Frederick-William Ì (1713–40), known as the 'sergeant-king', reverted to the policy of the Great Elector, building up a colossal army, setting the finances to rights, stripping the nobility of the last vestiges of independence and creating a centralized bureaucracy. The army was his obsession and his pride and joy was a notorious 'Regiment of giants', which he recruited (or kidnapped) from all over Europe. Frederick-William was honest, intelligent, immensely hard-working and God-fearing. He was also coarse, philistine and brutal, tendencies aggravated by an inherited disease, porphyria, which brought on terrifying and uncontrollable rages. Apart from when drilling his troops, he was never happier than when beer-swilling and smoking with his army cronies, pastimes which were despised by his wife, Sophia Dorothea of Hanover. She was sister of George II of England and a woman of some charm, but shallow, with artistic aspirations, and political ambitions for her children whom she hoped to marry to their English cousins.

Frederick as Crown Prince, 1712–40

Their son, the future Frederick the Great, was born at Berlin on 24 January 1712. As was customary, a French governess and tutor were assigned to teach him French, but not what Frederick-William called 'French ways', which the King abominated as effeminate and ungodly. Frederick's upbringing was therefore also entrusted to an eminent Prussian veteran, General von Finckenstein. The combination of influences, French and Prussian, was significant. Latin was expressly forbidden: Frederick was to be brought up as a good Protestant and to have nothing to do with Catholicism—'Anyone would have thought my father wanted me to be a theologian', he recalled.

Frederick-William's behaviour grew more neurotic and ferocious as his illness progressed. He was obsessed with the fear that his son would turn out to be an idle fop, and strove to coerce him, by terrifying scenes and physical beatings, into following his own model of Lutheran piety, barrack-square discipline, heavy drinking, smoking and hunting. Frederick, who was both sensitive and tough, reacted by demonstrating a taste for French literature, flute-playing and religious scepticism, a combination in which he was abetted by his mother and sister, Wilhelmine, and which was calculated to drive Frederick-William into further paroxysms. Frederick faced these paternal tantrums and assaults with icy self-control, masking his inner feelings with a profound disingenuousness, qualities that were later to mark his foreign policy methods: 'What goes on in that little head?', fumed Frederick-William.

Reduced to desperation by constant showdowns and humiliations, the eighteen-year-old Frederick conspired to flee abroad with a young friend, Lieutenant Katte. Frederick-William got wind of the plot at the last minute, imprisoned Frederick at Küstrin, and in a supreme effort to bring him to his senses, condemned Katte to death and forced Frederick to watch his friend being led to execution. As the blade fell, Frederick fainted.

Frederick-William now made his son undergo a thorough grounding in the running of the provincial government at Küstrin and, as colonel of a regiment, to take a proper interest in military affairs. Frederick at last put his back into the new regime with a mixture of energetic despair and a grudging recognition of his father's achievements in Prussia. Father and son were as reconciled as they ever could be and kept out of each other's way. In 1733, at his father's insistence, Frederick made a typical eighteenth-century dynastic match by marrying Elisabeth Christina of Brunswick-Bevern. The couple kept up separate households and the marriage was childless; throughout his life, Frederick treated his wife with callous disdain.

Having shown himself to be an obedient son, Frederick was allowed some sort of private life at his castle, a wedding-gift from his father, at Rheinsberg, north-west of Berlin. Frederick was to look back at the years spent here as the happiest of his life: he threw himself enthusiastically into reading, writing, music and theatricals, and he began his lifelong correspondence with Voltaire, who arranged the publication of Frederick's first work, the *Anti-Machiavel*. As for Gibbon, French for Frederick became a natural means of expression, and he spoke and wrote it more easily than German. From the *Anti-Machiavel* and from Frederick's way of life, it seemed that his reign would be that of a 'philosopher king', devoted to peace and the arts. Things turned out differently, however, when in August 1740 his father died and Frederick, at twenty-eight, became King of Prussia.

The grab for Silesia, 1740–48

Frederick's reign began with a flurry of liberal gestures: he reopened the Berlin Academy of Sciences, appointing the French scientist Maupertuis as its President; he disbanded the 'Regiment of Giants'; he abolished judicial torture; he proclaimed freedom of religion and of the press. He was very much aware, however, that under Frederick-William I Prussia, despite a well-stocked treasury and a disproportionately large army, had cut little ice in international affairs, being little more than a cat's paw of the Habsburgs. Frederick-William had stayed loyal to the Emperor Charles VI, who, having led him to understand that the Rhineland duchies of Jülich and Berg would go to Prussia, later double-crossed him. Frederick resolved to act differently from his father, believing that 'it is better to dupe than be duped'; he was indifferent to the Holy Roman Empire, except when it suited his purpose, and saw the Habsburgs simply as obstacles to Prussian expansionism.

His intentions suddenly revealed themselves, to Europe's astonishment, only two months after his accession. On the death of Charles VI, Frederick took advantage of the uncertainty over the Austrian succession (resulting from Charles's failure to leave a male heir) by invading the valuable Hapsburg province of Silesia, hoping that by a lightening campaign he could wrest it from Charles's daughter, Maria Theresa. His attack was against the advice of his generals, and, as Frederick admitted later, 'ambition, interest, the desire to make people talk about me, carried the day'. In the event, it took five years of hard fighting to secure Silesia, in the general European war which his action sparked off (the War of the Austrian Succession).

His baptism of fire at Mollwitz, near Breslau, in April 1741, was something of a fiasco. Frederick panicked and fled, owing victory, as he admitted, to the disciplined troops bequeathed by his father. He concluded a treaty with France in order to put pressure on the Austrians, and then betrayed the French to the Austrians in order to placate Maria Theresa. Unsuccessful in this ploy, he won his first personal victory at Chotusitz in Bohemia (May 1742), after which Maria Theresa reluctantly ceded Silesia by the Treaty of Breslau (June 1742). Frederick, having got what he wanted, returned in triumph to Berlin, leaving the French once more in the lurch.

Austrian successes in the larger European war, however, threatened his gains, and in 1744 he signed a fresh alliance with the French, and smashed the Austrians at Hohenfriedberg (June 1745) and Soor (September 1745). His hold on Silesia was confirmed by the Treaties of Dresden (1745) and Aix-la-Chapelle (1748).

Frederick the Great, 1746–56

The acquisition of Silesia increased Prussia's population by a half and her revenue by a third. It also thrust Prussia permanently into the cockpit of European politics. War revealed Frederick—now acclaimed as Frederick the Great—as a commander of unusual skill and daring, and a ruthless adept of power politics. He hoped for permanent peace, but he knew that Maria Theresa would not scruple to regain Silesia if she could, and that he must keep Prussia in a permanent state of military readiness—'always on alert' ('*toujours en vedette*') as he put it. To 'the consolidation of the state and the increase of its power' he showed a devotion every bit as zealous as his father's: the build-up and training of the army became his first priority—in ten years he doubled it, from 83 000 men to 150 000; the maintenance of sound finances to support it became his second priority, and the galvanization of society to the needs of the army, his third.

Figure 3   The Palace of Sans-Souci, Potsdam, built to Frederick's design (1745–7) by the architect G. W. von Knobelsdorff, in the full rococo style with caryatids by the sculptor F. C. Glume. At Frederick's insistence, the one-storey edifice opens directly on to the terrace, and hence does not occupy the commanding position over the grounds that Knobelsdorff had envisaged. Photograph by Paul Kafno.

Frederick's success was not due to original schemes of reform; in this he was far less creative than his father, being content on the whole to exploit the existing governmental machinery. What was extraordinary about Frederick was his combination of ferocious energy and cool analytical method: 'a well-run government must have a system as coherent as a system of philosophy', he wrote. He personally directed and supervised every aspect of government, whether from his desk at the palace of Sans-Souci (completed as his seat of government in 1747) or on the provincial inspection-tours which he undertook every spring, or, in war-time, from the battlefield itself.

The Seven Years War, 1756–63

In 1756 Prussia's position suddenly became extremely precarious, with the reversal by France and Austria of their centuries-old hostility. Maria Theresa, seeking to re-establish Habsburg influence in Germany and to regain Silesia, joined with France in a coalition aimed against Prussia and England. When Russia joined the coalition with a view to seizing East Prussia, Frederick found himself encircled by three vastly superior Powers, determined to 'clip his wings'. His only ally was Britain, and Britain's aim was to pick off French colonial possessions overseas while Frederick kept French troops tied down in Germany; British help therefore came mainly in the form of subsidies. Frederick sought to break out of encirclement by striking a pre-emptive blow at Saxony, which he duly knocked out of the war in the battle of Lobositz (October 1756).

Hopes of a quick end to the war by a few decisive victories were not fulfilled. Once again, Frederick's action unleashed a general European conflagration. In May 1757 he won a costly victory over the Austrians outside Prague, but, heavily outnumbered, his own forces suffered a shattering defeat at Kolin (June 1757). Henceforth, Frederick was forced strategically on to the defensive. Faced by successive invasions on all sides by large French, Austrian and Russian armies, he dashed from front to front, fighting desperately and heroically against overwhelming odds. He carried a phial of poison with him, having resolved in any event never to be taken alive, and never to surrender or sue for peace. Only his own unbending will and the consolations of music, literature and philosophy kept his spirits unbroken.

Tactically Frederick retained the upper hand, and used to the full his advantage of unified command to launch brilliant surprise attacks. In November 1757 he won a sensational victory in his best manner over the French at Rossbach, near Leipzig, and then a second, over the Austrians at Leuthen. Leuthen was the classic example of his 'oblique tactic'—attacking the enemy in force on his flank and rolling up his line before he could change front. After Rossbach the French concentrated their main attention on the British, but in the east, the Russians poured into Prussia in inexhaustible numbers. Frederick incurred terrible losses against them at Zorndorf (August 1758) where his 'oblique tactic' failed: the Russians stood firm in the face of murderous artillery fire. It was Europe's bloodiest battle of the century. Both sides claimed victory, while losing 20 000 men each; many more such 'victories' would ruin him. Two months later, Frederick was again defeated, this time by the Austrians at Hochkirch (October 1758); and on the very day of the battle he suffered the heaviest personal blow of his life in the death of his favourite sister, Wilhelmine.

The campaign of 1759 saw Frederick with a depleted force of raw recruits, his veteran officers and men all but wiped out. The battle of Kunersdorf against the Russians and Austrians (August 1759) was another bloodbath. 'The King', wrote one of his men, 'was always at the front crying: "Boys, don't desert me"; and at last he took a flag and said: "Whoever is a brave soldier, let him follow me!"' Two horses were shot under him and he would have met his death from a bullet had it not glanced off the gold snuff-box in his pocket. He was among the last to leave the field. With staring eyes and half-stunned, he cried: 'Is there no damn bullet for me, then?'

The following year he defeated the Austrians at Liegnitz (August 1760), but the Russians and Austrians occupied Berlin for a time. In November, he won another magnificent victory over the Austrians at Torgau, but ultimate catastrophe appeared inevitable. Continually urged by his friends to negotiate, he refused. Disaster was averted at the last minute by what he rightly called the 'miracle of the House of Hohenzollern'—the failure of the Russians to follow up their successes, the sudden death of the Empress Elisabeth of Russia in 1762, and the adoption of a pro-Prussian policy by her successor. Frederick was saved. Silesia was secured, this time permanently, at the peace of Hubertusburg in 1763.

'Der alte Fritz', 1763–86

The terrible strains of war, the death of his sister and of many friends, told on Frederick: at fifty, he looked an old man. 'I, who used to be as frisky as a young horse, bounding in a field, have become as slow as old Nestor, greying, eaten up with grief, riddled with infirmities.' His high spirits turned to sarcasm and cynicism. The remaining twenty-three years of his reign, perhaps the greatest period of his life, he devoted with grim, dogged determination to the vigorous restoration of his war-damaged kingdom, the reconstruction of her economy and finances, the encouragement of colonist immigration and land-reclamation by settlers from other parts of Germany, and, as ever, the maintenance of Prussia's armed strength as the pledge of her hard-won and still vulnerable Great Power status. 'If ever in my life I can do the state some service', he declared, 'it is now.'

Frederick's post-war achievements at least equalled his military feats. 'He performs miracles, though he believes in none', quipped a wag. He supervised the reform of the criminal law and the codification of Prussian law; he insisted on religious toleration and allowed freedom of speech. His passion for the rule of law and his revulsion at religious intolerance actually increased with age, as did his veneration of the ideal of the Prussian state.

Frederick's post-war diplomacy was perhaps still more brilliant than his victories and was certainly far less costly. In the Partition of 1772 he achieved the long-desired link between East Prussia and Brandenburg by a bloodless annexation of the Polish territory that separated them. When the Austrians sought to reassert their predominance in Germany by a plan to annex Bavaria he forced them to back down by military intervention (War of the Bavarian Succession, 1778–9); and in 1785, when Austria attempted to revive the scheme, he rallied the German princes to a diplomatic showdown and forced her to retreat a second time.

Frederick in old age was an increasingly solitary and indeed legendary figure. Amid the rococo charms of Sans-Souci, he slept on a simple camp-bed. Dressed in the same shabby uniform, boots and large cocked-hat— 'The King of Prussia

Figure 4   Administrative boundaries of Prussia in 1779. Prussia was 'a kingdom of border-strips', according to Voltaire.

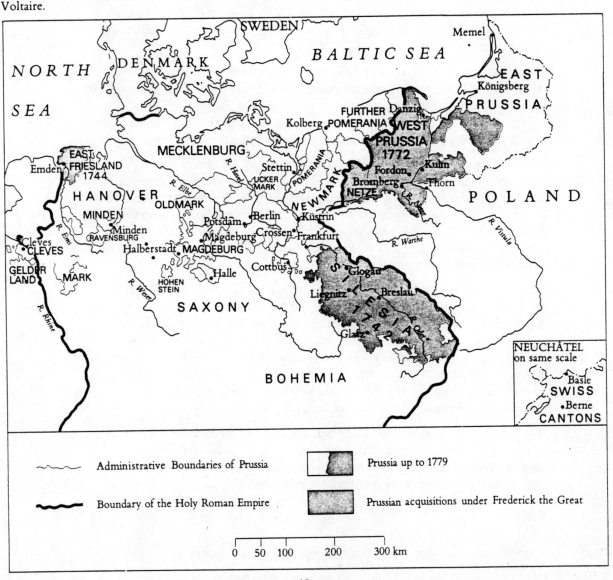

dresses plain', observed Dr Johnson in 1776, 'because the dignity of his character is sufficient'—Frederick went about his unchanging routine of administrative chores and inspections, year after year. Duty, self-sacrifice to the State, was the religion of this mocking free-thinker. Contrary to popular belief, he was generally candid and truthful—deviousness was reserved for his foreign policy. Indeed much of the hostility he aroused apparently stemmed from his unconventional refusal to don what he called 'the mask of hypocrisy'. He did not suffer fools kindly and had a low opinion of mankind, including his own subjects and his nephew and heir, the future Frederick-William II (in whose case it was amply justified). Yet to the select few he thought worthy of his indulgence, this sardonic pessimist could unbend to brilliant effect. At the dinner-table, he held forth on every subject under the sun: 'his conversation', wrote the Prince De Ligne, was 'encyclopaedic'. On such occasions, his charm was irresistible.

'The only creature to whom he showed gratitude', wrote Voltaire with malicious exaggeration, 'was the horse that carried him away from the battle of Mollwitz!' Certainly he kept his deeper emotions to himself, and the only creatures on which he openly lavished affection were his greyhounds. He did not care what people said of him. His veterans proudly called him '*Der alte Fritz*' ('Good old Fritz') but he scorned public acclaim and rarely descended to the kind of backslapping camaraderie that made Napoleon beloved among the ranks. On the contrary, no sooner was the Seven Years War over than he dismissed the non-noble officers whom he had reluctantly commissioned in the face of defeat and who had served him faithfully. 'The nobility', he explained, 'is the foundation and pillar of the State.' The common people he disdained as the *canaille* or riff-raff. At the same time, he was a stickler for justice, and acted decisively if he suspected that a poor man was being cheated out of his rights. 'The rich have many lawyers', he said, 'I am the advocate of the poor.'

Contemporary admirers saw his rule not as a crude tyranny, but as an inspiring example of what reasoned endeavour could achieve in the field of statemanship. His army was considered the best in Europe; his bureaucracy the most efficient, his system of justice the most uncorrupt. Prussia was seen, particularly by some of the French *philosophes*, as a haven of religious tolerance and free speech.

Frederick was regarded as the model of that unique late eighteenth-century phenonemon, the 'enlightened despot'.[5] He had no truck with representative institutions or constitutional government, seeing dynamic personal rule from above as essential for Prussia, and himself as 'the first servant of the State'. He expected the same selfless dedication from his subjects, and drove them like cattle. He died, in harness, at Sans-Souci, on 17 August 1786, aged seventy-four, and is buried next to his father in the Garrison Church at Potsdam.

Although Frederick built on the solid foundations laid down by his forbears, particularly his father, Prussia's spectacular bid for power in the eighteenth century was the result of his own single-minded ambition. He helped to smash the Holy Roman Empire, about which he was totally unsentimental; that institution was tottering anyway (and was finally laid to rest by Napoleon in 1806). By challenging Austria's political influence in Germany, he began a struggle for mastery which was to culminate a century later with the final defeat of Austria in 1866 and the unification of Germany under Prussian leadership in 1871.

The shape that unification was to take was also cast by Frederick, with his ready resort to aggression, his militarization of society, his social conservatism and his ideological alignment (arising from the partition of Poland) with autocratic Russia and Austria, rather than with the liberal-constitutional West.

[5] Others included Catherine II of Russia, Joseph II of Austria, Gustav III of Sweden (Frederick's nephew) and Charles III of Spain.

German nationalists of the nineteenth and twentieth century have hailed Frederick as a kindred spirit, 'the patron saint of Germany', which would have amused that cosmopolitan francophile, who destroyed whatever fragile bonds of German unity existed. Western liberals denounce him as the embodiment of Prussian militarism. Certainly, Prussian society retained many Frederician hallmarks right up to 1945. But as for statesmanship and personality, while some comparison with Bismarck may be apt, it is hard to see any affinity between Hitler—that semi-literate demagogue, a vulgarian to the bootstraps, whose ideas were the drunken babble of the Bavarian beer-house writ large—and the monarch who, had he never been king, would still have been an ornament of civilized society; whose intelligence was respected by the most discriminating minds of Europe; and who used his royal power to abolish torture, to curtail capital punishment, to impose the rule of law, to grant freedom of thought and religion to everyone, and toleration to the Jews. The Prince De Ligne, one of the most sophisticated of eighteenth-century diplomats, a man of the world, not prone to exaggerate, called Frederick 'the greatest man who ever lived', and on hearing of his death, said he no longer believed that comets appeared on Caesar's death, since none were seen at Frederick's.

Frederick retained Prussia's basic administrative structure—a hierarchy of executive boards—as created by his father, but he exploited its potential to the full. His system was the zenith of what was called 'cabinet rule', not in the English sense of government by the king's ministers, but in quite the opposite sense of personal rule by the king himself from his 'cabinet', or study at Sans-Souci. This was the nerve-centre of the administration, from where Frederick alone formulated policy, coordinated the work of the various branches of government, issued directives or 'cabinet orders' to his so-called 'ministers' and supervised their implementation.

The advantage of the system was its amazing rapidity. Frederick acted with unremitting energy, detailed knowledge of the matters in hand, decisiveness and a

Figure 5 Frederick's desk in his study at Sans-Souci. Both the writing table, *c* 1746—height 80 cm (31½ ins)—and the cartonnier, or document cabinet, *c* 1746—height 242 cm (95½ ins)—are ascribed to Gaudreau with gilt bronze mounts by Caffiéri. Compare with Plate 14 in the Colour Book. Photograph by Paul Kafno.

strict, military precision, undistracted by family or court life. He kept his bureau-cracy, probably the most efficient in Europe, under tight control, forbidding any individual initiative and personally checking its activities by annual tours of inspection. No one man could fully control everything, of course, and there is evidence, at least towards the end of the reign, of officials colouring their reports to fit what they thought Frederick wanted to hear. Likewise, his on-the-spot visits were less effective in outlying districts (he never visited East Prussia after the Seven Years War) than in Brandenburg itself. Even so, his achievement remains extraordinary. It depended on quite exceptional qualities in the ruler and what Frederick regarded as a new philosophy of kingship. Documents 1–4 illustrate his defence of 'enlightened absolutism' as opposed to monarchy on the French or British pattern.

1   Frederick II on enlightened absolutism

Confidential memorandum intended for the use of his heir; 1752

('Testament politique' (1752) in G. B. Volz (ed) *Die Politischen Testamente Friedrichs des Grossen* (1920), Berlin, pp. 37–9)

In a State like this, the ruler must necessarily take charge of things personally, because, if he is wise, he will pursue only the public interest, which is his own; whereas a minister always has his mind on things which further his own interests; and instead of promoting deserving candidates, appoints his own creatures and strives to consolidate his own position through the number of people whom he makes dependent on him.

The monarch on the other hand will support the nobility, keep the clergy within its proper bounds, will not allow the princes of the blood to intrigue or plot, and will reward merit without those partisan views which ministers secretly entertain in everything they do.

But if it is vital that the ruler should personally direct the internal affairs of his State, how much more vital it is for him to conduct his foreign policy in person, to form the alliances which suit him, to make his own decisions in critical and awkward situations. Finances, domestic government, foreign policy and military affairs are so closely connected that it is impossible to deal with one of these branches in isolation from the others. When that happens, rulers do badly. In France, four ministers rule the kingdom: the Ministers of Finance, Marine, War and Foreign Affairs. These four 'kings' never agree or concur; hence all the contradictions which we see in the French government: one man reverses out of jealousy the policy promoted by another abler man; no system; no planning; chance rules all, and everything in France is the result of court intrigues; the English know everything that is discussed at Versailles; there is no secrecy and consequently no proper foreign policy.

A well-run government must have a system as coherent as a system of philosophy; all the measures taken must be well reasoned; finances, foreign policy and military affairs must work to the same end, namely the consolidation of the State and the increase of its power. Now a system can only emanate from one mind; and this must be the monarch's. Idleness, luxury or stupidity prevent rulers from pursuing the noble task of bringing about their people's happiness. Such monarchs make themselves so contemptible that they become the laughing-stock of their contemporaries, and as far as history is concerned, their role is, at best, to mark a chronological period. They vegetate on the throne, unworthy to occupy it, intent on self-indulgence. Their negligence towards their peoples even becomes criminal. A monarch is not raised to this lofty rank or entrusted with supreme power in order to live in luxury, to grow fat on the people's substance and enjoy himself while everyone else suffers. The monarch is the first servant of the State. He is well paid in order that he may maintain the dignity of his rank; but he is required to contribute actively to the good of the State, and to direct its principal policies conscientiously, at the least. Certainly he needs assistance; to master all the details is too much for him; but he must listen to everyone's complaints and have justice promptly done to potential victims of oppression. A woman came to petition a king of Epirus, who impatiently told her to leave him in peace: 'Why are you king, then', she retorted, 'if not to do me justice?' A fine observation, which rulers should bear constantly in mind.

2 Frederick II on enlightened absolutism

Confidential memorandum intended for the use of his heir; 1776

('Exposé du gouvernement prussien', *Oeuvres de Frédéric le Grand* Vol IX (1848), Berlin, pp. 190–1)

In foreign policy, we should look to the future as far as possible and ascertain future turns of events in Europe, whether to form alliances or to thwart the plans of our enemies. We should not believe that we can shape events; but when they present themselves, we must seize them in order to exploit them. That is why finances must be in order, so that the government is ready to act the moment political considerations indicate that the time is ripe. War itself should be waged according to political principles, in order to inflict the bloodiest blow on the enemy . . .

From what I have just said, it is clear that foreign policy, military affairs and finances are so intimately connected that they cannot be separated. They must all be coordinated simultaneously, and their joint effect, if operated according to sound rules of policy, will bring the greatest benefit to States. In France, there is a 'king' in charge of each individual branch of government, namely, the chief minister, whether of finances, war or foreign affairs. There is no focal point, and these branches, lacking unity, diverge: each minister is concerned only with the details of his own department and there is no-one to coordinate their efforts towards one fixed object. If a similar thing happened in this State, it would be destroyed; for large kingdoms advance together with their abuses and maintain themselves by their weight and their intrinsic strength, while small states are quickly crushed, unless they are active, vigorous and dynamic.

These are a few of my reflections and ideas on the government of this country, which, until it acquires far greater strength and better frontiers, must be ruled by monarchs who are always alert, wary of their neighbours and ready to defend themselves from one day to the next against their enemies' designs.

Exercise

Why does Frederick regard absolutism as indispensable in Prussia?

Specimen answer

Firstly, because in his view only one man, the monarch, is sufficiently disinterested to follow 'national' policies rather than personal or sectarian interests. Note the contrast with France. (See Units 13–14, *The Encyclopédie,* Section 1.) Secondly, because the absolute primacy of foreign policy in Prussia necessitates a single overview of 'finances, domestic government, foreign policy and military affairs' until Prussia 'acquires far greater strength and better frontiers'.

Exercise

What justification for absolutism does document 2 add to document 1?

Discussion

It stresses Frederick's conviction of the primacy of foreign policy in Prussia and the need to coordinate it with domestic policy. Throughout his reign, even after the triumphs of the Seven Years War, he was constantly concerned with Prussia's vulnerability. He sought a status for Prussia comparable with that of the Great Powers—England, France, Austria and Russia—but knew that he could achieve it only by dint of a disproportionate strain and the maintenance of a huge army. A full defeat in war would result in Prussia's disappearance as a sovereign state.

3 Frederick II on enlightened absolutism

Published essay; 1777

('Essai sur les formes du gouvernement et sur les devoirs des souverains', *Oeuvres de*

Frédéric le Grand Vol IX (1848), Berlin pp. 198–210)

The citizens only granted pre-eminence to one of their fellows in return for the services which they expected from him. These services consist in upholding the laws, ensuring that justice is scrupulously observed, opposing the corruption of manners as far as he can and defending the State against its enemies. The ruler must supervise agriculture, he must ensure abundant supplies for the community and promote industry and trade. He is like a sentry, permanently on guard against his neighbours and the activities of the enemies of the State. . .Just as all the springs of a watch operate to the same purpose, namely, to measure time, so too the springs of government should be set in such a way that all the different parts of the administration contribute equally to the greatest good of the State, that vital object that must never be lost sight of. . .

The ruler is linked by indissoluble bonds to the body of the State; consequently he feels the repercussion of all the ills that afflict his subjects, and likewise, society suffers the misfortunes which affect its ruler. There is only one good, namely, that of the State in general. If the ruler loses some provinces, he is no longer in the same position as before to assist his subjects. If misfortune has driven him into debt, it is the poor citizens who must pay; on the other hand, if the population is very small, if the people languishes in poverty, the ruler lacks every resource. These are truths so incontrovertible that there is no need to stress them further. I repeat, then, the ruler represents the State; he and his people form a single body which can only be happy as long as they are both harmoniously united. The ruler is to the society he governs what the head is to the whole body; he must see, think and act for the whole community, in order to obtain for it all the benefits of which it is capable. If monarchical government is to be superior to republican, the monarch's decision is all-important; he must be active and upright, and must muster all his good qualities in order to fulfil his destined career. This is my idea of his duties. He must acquire an accurate and detailed knowledge of his country's strengths and weaknesses, including monetary resources, population, finances, trade and the laws and character of the nation which he is to rule. . . Since any individual who fails to act according to principle is inconsistent in his conduct, it is all the more important that the ruler, who is responsible for the people's welfare, should act according to a fixed system of politics, war, finances, trade and law. . .

These are the general duties that a ruler must carry out. In order not to fall short of them he must constantly remind himself that he is a man, like the least of his subjects; if he is society's first judge, first general, first financier, first minister, it is not in order that he should merely symbolize their duties, but that he should carry them out. He is the first servant of the State, obliged to act with probity, wisdom, and complete dis-interestedness, as if at any moment he were accountable to his citizens for his stewardship. So he is to blame, if he squanders the national revenue, which is the product of taxation, on luxury, ostentation and dissipation, when he should be promoting good moral conduct, which is the guardian of the laws, when he should be improving national education, and not undermining it by his bad example. . . This is the true idea that should be held of the duties of a monarch and is the only way to make monarchical government good and beneficial. If many rulers behave differently, we must attribute this to their lack of reflection on the institution of monarchy and the duties attaching to it. They have assumed a responsibility whose onerousness and importance they have underestimated; they have erred through lack of knowledge; for in our day ignorance causes more errors than wickedness.

This portrait of a monarch will perhaps seem in the eyes of critics to resemble the ideal of the Sage depicted by the Stoics, an ideal which has never existed in fact, and to which Marcus Aurelius alone came closest.

Exercise

What differences, if any, do you note between Frederick's view of monarchy and the view epitomized by Louis XIV in France? (See Units 13–14, *The Encyclopédie*, Section 1.)

Discussion

To Louis, the king was a law unto himself, accountable to no one but God, whose representative he was. This view was neatly summed up in the famous remark attributed to Louis—'*L'état—c'est moi*' ('The state? *I* am the state'). The king's will was law, and no matter how arbitrary, oppressive, unjust or irrational it might be (as Louis' reign came to be seen, particularly towards the end because of his long wars and the persecution of the Huguenots), the king was above criticism, because he was 'the Lord's anointed'. This theory of the 'divine right' of kings had been popular in England under the Stuarts in the seventeenth century, but in the eighteenth, under the Hanoverians, it was subscribed to only by the Jacobites, who supported the exiled Stuarts. Indeed it could hardly be invoked by the supporters of the Hanoverians, who were manifestly kings by Act of Parliament rather than by the grace of God. Rather, it was argued after the 'Glorious Revolution' of 1688 that the Stuarts had been rightly deprived of the throne because they had failed to measure up to certain basic standards of fitness, or, as the Whig philosopher, John Locke (see Units 8–9, p. 17), argued, they had failed to observe the conditions of an implied agreement between king and people: this was the so-called 'Social Contract', whereby the people were deemed to have granted power to the king not unconditionally, but in return for certain services that they expected from him. In France the divine right theory continued to be invoked in the eighteenth century; it underlay Louis XV's famous show-down with the Paris *Parlement* in 1766 (the *séance de la flagellation*). In Prussia, Frederick-William had stoutly defended it, insisting that 'Salvation is God's; everything else is mine', and 'We are King and Master and can do whatever we please'. Frederick, a religious sceptic, scorned to justify his rule in terms of divine right. He abandoned the traditional ceremonial and hieratic aspects of kingship. He refused a coronation: 'a crown', he observed, 'is just a hat that lets in the rain'. At Sans-Souci there were no levées, religious or court ceremonial, as there were at Versailles: Frederick went about his business without fuss or parade, invariably dressed in a shabby military uniform, showing that he was 'a man, like the least of his subjects'.

Invoking the Social Contract theory—'the citizens only granted pre-eminence to one of their fellows in return for the services which they expected from him'—he argued that the sole justification for the monarch's existence was his compliance with the interests of the State. The State was no longer seen as simply a private chattel, which the king could deal with as he liked, but rather as akin to a trust property, which the king must manage conscientiously on behalf of his subjects—'the king is the first servant of the state'. By listing the qualities necessary in the ruler—decisiveness, energy, integrity, etc—and by criticizing rulers who fail to meet these ideals, Frederick is implicitly laying down objective standards against which the king, immune from criticism according to the divine right notions, could be measured 'as if at any moment he were accountable to his citizens for his stewardship'. It was not that Frederick believed that kings should be really accountable to their subjects, as under 'constitutional' monarchy in England (where the king could levy taxes and raise armed forces only with Parliament's consent); but he argued that monarchy, like other institutions, was subject to criticism, and was no longer self-justifying. By claiming that a monarch 'is a man, like the least of his subjects', Frederick, as Goethe observed, helped to undermine one of the props of monarchy, its mystery and sacrosanctity. Frederick's aim, however, was not to lessen respect for the institution of monarchy, but to stress that the monarch must justify his existence by his devotion to the state.

Exercise

What does Frederick see as the king's most important duty?

Discussion

He refers several times to the 'people's happiness', 'the public interest', justice, the promotion of agriculture, industry and trade. But he was less concerned with the actual needs of the people, the wishes they might have expressed if given the opportunity, than the interests of the State, 'the greatest good of the State':

'There is only one good—that of the State in general', dictated by objective necessity as revealed by reason and perceived by the ruler. The intensity of this concept represents something new and directly related to the Enlightenment cult of Reason. In the words of Frederick's German biographer, Gerhard Ritter:

> In Frederick's state neither the personal interest of the prince and his dynasty, nor the desires of his subjects ultimately decided the government's actions. Domestic and foreign policy were guided exclusively by *raison d'état*, by the interests of the state. Both prince and people were its servants. Never before or again was the concept of state individuality and state interest grasped so clearly—and with almost abstract purity—and never was it as politically effective as in Frederick's enlightened despotism.
>
> Gerhard Ritter *Frederick the Great: an Historical Profile*, trans. by Peter Paret (1968), University of California Press, p. 70

Figure 6   Sans-Souci, the Little Gallery. 'I am a philosopher by inclination, a politician out of duty' (Frederick the Great). The Little Gallery houses six Roman busts (part classical, part eighteenth-century), classical statues of gods (acquired from the Polignac collection, 1742), paintings by pupils of Watteau and French chandeliers with rock-crystal hangings. Photograph by Paul Kafno.

Frederick took personal charge of finances, reducing his 'ministers' to little more than accountants, responsible for individual areas of revenue and finance, but without knowledge, let alone control, of the overall budget. Income and expenditure remained the King's secret; and Frederick managed them with method and probity: Prussia was the only major continental state to balance its budgets and produce a growing surplus. Her revenue in 1762 was as great as Russia's, with a *per capita* basis of taxation no greater than Austria's and much less than that of France. Frederick's one extravagance was his palaces at Sans-Souci which he paid for from the revenues of his own crown estates. His stand against the wanton extravagance indulged in at public expense by several German courts, such as Saxony, and Prussia itself under Frederick I (1688–1713), earned him a reputation for miserliness.

4 Frederick II on thrift

Confidential memorandum intended for the use of his heir; 1752

('Testament politique' (1752) in G. B. Volz (ed) *Die Politischen Testamente Friedrichs des Grossen* (1920), Berlin, pp. 35–6)

I think that it is as little proper for a ruler to be miserly as to be a spendthrift; but he should be economical as well as generous: economical because he is the administrator of the State's property. The money he receives represents the people's blood and sweat, and he must use it for the good of the whole community. To misspend this money in peacetime and to be short of large sums in war, to dissipate all your revenue without looking ahead and to have to oppress the people with new taxes when the State finds itself the victim of aggression, is to act insanely and more like a tyrant than a father of the people. A statesman should never say: 'I did not think that such-and-such a thing would happen'; his task is to foresee everything and be prepared for anything.

Now in this country, which is entirely self-supporting, he who rules it must not be slow to realize that he has no pecuniary resources beyond those which he can get by accumulating them in peacetime. He must therefore be deaf to public gossip and despise its worthless opinions. Suppose the public accuses you of being miserly or niggardly, what does it matter? It judges according to false ideas and would share your opinion if you told it of your reasons. You must follow your own system, once it is well founded, without allowing yourself to be distracted in your path by the chatter of crickets or the croaking of frogs.

5 Frederick II on enlightened absolutism

Published essay; 1779

('Lettres sur l'amour de la patrie', *Oeuvres de Frédéric le Grand* Vol IX (1848), Berlin, pp. 216–7)

I remember you were of the opinion that one might expect to find true citizens in republics, but that you thought there were none in monarchies. Let me disabuse you of this error. Good monarchies, where the administration is wise and full of mildness, constitute in our day a form of government which is closer to oligarchy than to despotism, for it is the laws alone that rule. Let us go into some detail. Consider the number of persons employed on the advisory committees, in the administration of justice and of finances, in diplomatic missions abroad, in commerce, in the armed forces, in the internal civilian administration; add to this those who have a voice in the provinces; all of them, let me inform you, share a part of the sovereign authority. So the ruler is not a despot ruling merely according to his own whim; he should be seen as the focal point where all the radii of the circle converge. This form of government provides in its deliberations the secrecy which is lacking in republics; and the various branches of the administration, being interconnected, advance together like the four-horse chariots of the Romans, and operate in combination for the general welfare of the people. Moreover, you will always find less of the spirit of party faction in monarchies, if they have at their head a firm ruler, than in republics, which are often torn apart by citizens who intrigue and plot to overthrow one another. If there is in Europe an exception to what I have just been saying, it is perhaps the Ottoman Empire or some other government which, failing to recognize its true interest, has failed to bind closely enough the interests of the individuals with those of the monarch. A well-ruled kingdom should be like a family, of which the monarch is the father, and the citizens his children; their good and bad fortune are shared between them, for the monarch cannot be happy when his people are wretched. When this union is well established, duty and gratitude produce good citizens: their identification with the State is absolute; they cannot dissociate themselves from it; they would have everything to lose and nothing to gain.

You require examples? The government of Sparta was oligarchic and it produced a host of great patriots. Rome, after she lost her freedom, furnishes you with an Agrippa, a Thrasea Paetus, a Helvidius Priscus, a Corbulo, an Agricola,[6] emperors like Titus, Marcus Aurelius, Trajan and Julian: in a word, a large number of those masculine and virile men who put the interests and the advantage of the public good before their own.

Figure 7 'My good old Emperor Marcus Aurelius' (Frederick the Great). This classical bust of Marcus Aurelius, acquired from the Polignac collection, 1742, is at Sans-Souci. Photograph by Paul Kafno.

Exercise

How does Frederick distinguish enlightened absolute rule from outright 'despotism?'

[6] Agrippa was Augustus's right-hand man. Thrasea Paetus, a Stoic, was condemned to death for his republican opposition under Nero and committed suicide; Helvidius Priscus, his son-in-law, was exiled and later executed for his opposition to Vespasian; Corbulo, a successful general, recalled by Nero on suspicion of treason, committed suicide. Agricola, Governor of Britain, was father-in-law of the historian Tacitus, who wrote his biography. Compare Gibbon's more critical view of the effects of imperial rule on individual virtue (e.g. Agricola and Corbulo, Course Anthology Vol 1 p. 186).

He makes a point of distinguishing the benevolent absolutism of 'good monarchies, where the administration is wise and full of mildness' from 'despotism'. The distinction is to be found first of all in the existence of the rule of law—'it is the laws alone that rule'. Next, it is to be found in the administrative, military and judicial bodies, which 'share a part of the sovereign authority', so that 'the ruler is not a despot ruling merely according to his own whim', but 'the focal point, where all the radii of the circle converge'. (For a closer critical look at the question of the rule of law in Prussia, see section 4.)

The Antonines and the 'Old Romans' should be familiar to you from Units 10–12 *Gibbon's Decline and Fall of the Roman Empire* (pp. 21–26). Why do you suppose that Frederick brings them into his discussion of kingship?

These classical echoes represent another defence of absolutism from the charge of 'despotism'. Frederick subscribes to the view that *humanitas* and political integrity, conventionally seen as typically 'republican' virtues, are compatible with an absolutist system of government, which can produce benevolent rulers, like the Antonines, or staunch opponents of despotism, like Thrasea Paetus etc. (For Gibbon's more critical view, see Units 10–12.)

Another stoic theme underlying Frederick's philosophy of kingship is the paramountcy of duty. Frederick explicitly rejects the epicurean doctrine that man is born for happiness and has a right to 'exist in the obscurity of private life'. On the contrary, the best rulers follow the stoic ethic of what Gibbon calls 'active virtue': they 'put the interests and the advantage of the public before their own'. The supreme example of Frederick's call for self-sacrifice comes in the next document, a cabinet-order written at the beginning of the Seven Years War.

6 *Frederick II on enlightened absolutism*

Secret cabinet order from Frederick II to Count Finckenstein★; 10 January 1757

(*Oeuvres de Frédéric le Grand* Vol XXV (1854), Berlin, p. 320)

Should it be my fate to be taken prisoner, I forbid anyone to entertain the slightest concern for my person, or to pay the least attention to anything I might write from my place of confinement. If such a misfortune should befall me, I shall sacrifice myself for the State, and everyone must then obey my brother. I shall hold him and all my ministers and generals responsible on pain of death for seeing that neither a province nor a ransom is offered for my release, but that the war is continued and every advantage seized, just as if I had never existed.

★ Prussian Foreign Minister during the Seven Years War

2 State and Society

A military state

By far the most important single institution in Prussia since the Great Elector (Frederick-William, 1640–88) was the army. Its growth in the eighteenth century, and particularly under Frederick, was phenomenal: from 40 000 to 80 000 men under Frederick-William I, and from 150 000 in 1763 to over 200 000 by 1786. This was fraught with implications for Prussia and Europe. At any one time, nearly five per cent of Prussia's population was under arms, an astonishingly high proportion for the time, imposing enormous strains on society and the economy. Everything was rigidly subordinated to military needs, and the whole character of the State became militarized under Frederick. The French statesman Mirabeau, who visited Prussia at the end of the reign, observed: 'Most states have an army; Prussia is the only case of an army having a state'. Prussian 'militarism' has traditionally provoked adverse comment from English historians as the embodiment of mindless regimentation and the pursuit of brute force, power and aggression as the ends of government.

1   Frederick II on statecraft

Confidential memorandum intended for the use of his heir; 1752

('Testament politique' (1752) in G. B. Volz (ed) *Die Politischen Testamente Friedrichs des Grossen* (1920), Berlin, p. 27)

For monarchs there are two sides to government: one concerns internal rule, and consists of the interests of the State and the maintenance of the system of government; the other extends to the whole European system, and works to consolidate the security of the State and to maximize (by customary and legitimate means) the number of the ruler's possessions, his power and his reputation.

2   Frederick II on war and society

Confidential memorandum intended for the use of his heir; 1776

('Exposé du gouvernement prussien', *Oeuvres de Frédéric le Grand* Vol IX (1848), Berlin, p. 186)

The geographical position of the State obliges us to maintain many troops: for our neighbours are Austria, Russia, France and Sweden. 220 000 men are kept on a war footing, including special batallions and auxiliary cavalry. Of this number, 180 000 men could be put in the field; but the moment it becomes necessary to raise three armies, it is obvious that we do not have many troops in comparison with our neighbours. I think that the discipline and tactics that have been introduced should remain on their present footing, provided that there is no change in the system of waging war; for then there is no alternative but to adapt to circumstances and change with them. But to equal or surpass the enemy, one must act in an orderly and disciplined fashion and encourage and reward the officers, so that noble emulation spurs them on to surpass the enemy. If the monarch does not personally participate in military affairs and if he fails to set the example, all is lost. If idle courtiers are preferred to military men, everyone will be seen to prefer idleness to the soldier's laborious profession, and so, instead of our officers being noblemen, recourse will have to be had to commoners, which would be the first step towards military decadence and decline.

Exercise

What do documents 1–2 suggest about the character of Frederick's brand of 'militarism'?

They suggest that Frederick was concerned with political stability—'the maintenance of the system of government' and the increase in the territorial acquisitions and political power of the State. In other words, conservatism at home (note his derogatory remarks about 'commoners') and expansion abroad.

While Frederick believed in the necessity of a large army and in the ruler's personal participation in military affairs, he seems to have been motivated less by a desire for personal 'glory' in the manner of Louis XIV (except, perhaps, in the case of his invasion of Silesia in 1740) than by his acute anxiety over Prussia's basic and inherent weakness as compared with her neighbours. To him, 'militarism' was a necessity for a small, underpopulated and overextended state; and his response to the chronic external threat was to build up a huge permanent standing army, both as a deterrent and a means of defence. 'Militarism' in Frederick's view was an integral necessity of State, dictated by geography and political reality, not simply an expression of personal vainglory, or a desire of war for war's sake. (See also section 7.)

The nobility

Frederick's social policy was one of rigid class stratification and immobility. He regarded the nobility as 'the foundation and pillar of the state' and a natural governing elite. His prejudices in this respect and his disdain for low birth were strongly marked, and compared with the Great Elector and Frederick-William I, both of whom had recruited non-nobles to serve in the army and bureaucracy, Frederick's policy was literally 'reactionary'. He reserved the officer ranks in the army and administration for nobles (to a degree stricter even than was the case in France; see Units 13–14, *The Encyclopédie*); and when forced by the crippling casualties of the Seven Years War to grant temporary commissions to non-nobles, he was quick to weed them out once the war was over, preferring non-Prussians with the requisite number of quarterings to native commoners. All his thirty-four generals in 1740 were nobles; and in 1804, out of 422 staff-officers, only two were non-noble. Frederick consolidated and increased the privileges of the nobles. They were already exempt from taxation in most provinces. He jealously protected their monopoly of land ownership, subsidizing them with special State mortgages and outright gifts, and introduced an entail system to preserve their estates intact. The basic role of the Prussian nobility and its predominance in state and society, established by Frederick and cemented in the Seven Years War, was to last at least until 1918. Stripped of all independent|political power by Frederick-William I, its ambitions were channelled under Frederick into unquestioning devotion to king and State.

3 *Frederick II on the nobility*

Confidential memorandum intended for the use of his heir; 1752

('Testament politique' (1752) in G. B. Volz (ed) *Die Politischen Testamente Friedrichs des Grossen* (1920), Berlin, pp. 29–30)

One object of the policy of the ruler of this State is to support its nobility: for whatever may befall, it may perhaps have a wealthier nobility, but never one more valiant or loyal. In order to guarantee them in their ownership of land, it is essential to prevent commoners from acquiring estates belonging to the nobility, and to persuade commoners to invest their capital in trade; so that if some noble is obliged to sell his lands, the only purchasers are nobles. It is likewise essential to prevent the nobility from serving abroad, and to inspire them with *esprit de corps* and patriotism. This has been my|constant endeavour, and throughout the first war [War of the Austrian Succession, 1740–8] I took all possible steps to make the name of Prussians well known, to teach all the officers that, whatever

Figure 8 Daniel Chodowiecki (in the style of Watteau), *Gathering in the Tiergarten*, oil on canvas, Berlin, Ullstein GMBH Bilderdienst. 'Conduct unbefitting an officer, such as drunkenness, or patronage of low coffee-houses and brothels, must not be tolerated; nor must officers be allowed to consort with common people or members of the *bourgeoisie*, but must confine themselves to the society of their equals or superiors' (Frederick the Great).

province they might come from, they were all regarded as Prussians, and hence that all these provinces, though geographically separate, form a single unit. It is right that the nobility should choose to devote its services to its own country rather than to any other. For this reason, strict laws have been laid down against nobles who have gone to serve elsewhere without permission.

Exercise ══

Are Frederick's views in document 3 merely an expression of aristocratic prejudice? Or have they also an objective basis?

Discussion ═══

I think it can be argued that Frederick was not so much star-struck by high birth for its own sake, nor did he believe that great qualities were necessarily hereditary: it was rather that the Junkers (Prussian nobles) were *in any case* the natural leaders over the peasants, whom they ruled on their estates. Certainly he also held that they were uniquely fitted by breeding and outlook to officer the army and

29

bureaucracy; like Fielding and Gibbon, Frederick evidently regarded *humanitas* as the birthright of the well-born (see Units 10–12 section 5, 'A Note on *Humanitas*', p. 20), but note that Frederick demanded obedience, courage and self-sacrifice, *not* advice.

Note that Frederick's aristocratic predilections were far from untypical of the age. Compare, for example, these comments on the Prussian officers by a German observer, (admittedly, himself a nobleman) J. C. von Riesbeck, who visited Prussia in the 1770s:

> Another cause, which, in my opinion, greatly contributes to the excellence of the army, is the high birth of the officers. They are most of them of the first nobility of the country. . . They must all have been educated at the cadets' school and have served as cadets. I have some very respectable acquaintances among them. They are in every respect well-educated people, and upon the whole very sensible men. The small pay of the subalterns obliges them to be economical, which is great advantage to the service. They have all a martial appearance, and that alacrity in everything, which bespeaks men always ready to cut a knot with their swords.
>
> *Travels through Germany, translated by Mr Maty*, Vol III (1787), London, p. 22

The peasantry

The heaviest burdens in Prussia (as in France) were borne by the peasants. They provided the overwhelming majority of army recruits. They bore the bulk of direct taxation, which has been calculated on average as amounting to some forty per cent of the average peasant's net income. They were obliged to provide billeting for officials and troops in transit and to undertake road works, canal construction etc, as well as to perform feudal services for the noble landowners. Frederick indeed called them 'the beasts of burden of human society'.

The degrees of peasant dependence on the landlord varied widely across Prussia: west of the Elbe, there were freehold or tenant farmers performing various customary services, but legally free; east of the Elbe, conditions became progressively harsher. Freeholders were rare: there were 'protected' peasants, performing services, but free to leave the estate, and serfs, bound to the land and hereditable. In East Prussia, the most numerous class consisted of casual farm labourers, legally free, employed by the nobleman and provided by him with a cottage and a few acres, from which they could, however, be dispossessed by him at will.

4 Frederick II on the peasants

Confidential memorandum intended for the use of his heir; 1752

('Testament politique' (1752) in G. B. Volz (ed) *Die Politischen Testamente Friedrichs des Grossen* (1920), Berlin, pp. 30–31)

I have freed the peasants from some of the services which they performed in the past; instead of serving six days a week, as they used to, they have only three days of *corvée*.* This measure has stirred up the peasants of the nobility who in many places have rebelled against their masters. The monarchy should hold a balance between peasant and noble, to prevent them from ruining each other. In Silesia, apart from Upper Silesia, the condition of the peasant is very good; in Upper Silesia, he is a serf. Some day efforts will have to be made to emancipate him. I have set the example on my own estates where I have started placing them on the same footing as those in Lower Silesia. However peasants should be prevented from buying lands belonging to nobles, and nobles from buying peasant land, because peasants cannot serve as officers in the army, and the nobles, by enclosing peasant holdings, would diminish the number of settlers and farmers.

* Obligatory work for the landowner

5 Frederick II on serfdom in Pomerania

Cabinet order to Privy Finance-Councillor von Brenckenhoff*; 23 May 1763

(R. Stadelmann (ed) *Preussens Könige in ihrer Thätigkeit für die Landescultur*, Part II, *Friedrich der Grosse* (1882), Leipzig, p. 340)

All forms of serfdom, whether in royal, noble or municipal villages, are henceforth absolutely and unequivocally abolished; and all who may seek to oppose this should be made to realize, if possible peacefully, but in the case of resistance, by force, that these settled ideas of His Majesty are directed to the needs of the whole province in its work.

* Official in charge of land reclamation

6 Frederick II on the peasants

Published essay; 1777

('Essai sur les formes du gouvernement', *Oeuvres de Frédéric le Grand* Vol IX (1848), Berlin, p. 205–6)

The monarch must frequently remind himself of the state of the poor: he should put himself in the place of a peasant or a manual worker and say to himself: 'If I had been born in the class of citizens whose hands constitute their capital, what would I wish the monarch to do?' . . .

In most European states there are provinces where the peasants are tied to the soil as their masters' serfs. Of all conditions this is the most wretched and the most repugnant to humanity. Certainly, no man was born to be the slave of his fellow; we rightly detest such an abuse, and we imagine that all that would be required is the wish to abolish this barbarous custom. But this is not the case; serfdom is the result of ancient contracts made between landowners and peasants. Agriculture is established on the basis of peasant services; if we sought to abolish in one blow this abominable mode of procedure, we would completely upset the agricultural system, and it would be necessary to indemnify the nobility for the loss of income which it would suffer.

7 Peasant status in Prussia

Statute from Frederick's *Code of Law*; published posthumously 1794

(In *Code général pour les états prussiens* Vol II (year ix), Paris, pp. 319–20)

It could not be the aim of the new legislation to abolish entirely these distinctions, to place the peasant from East Prussia on a completely equal footing with the peasant from the district of Magdeburg or Cleves, and thus to cut the Gordian knot at one blow. This could not be done without violating rights justly acquired and which must be sacred to the State, or without upsetting established laws and occasioning violent disruptions to the welfare of the two classes, which are more closely united by a mutual bond than is commonly believed. Such a violent operation is all the more unnecessary in that the law has already taken care in Prussia to abolish slavery and excessive servitude, with their dishonourable consequences for human nature; to stipulate that serfs may possess and acquire personal property as well as all other citizens; and to protect them, through the laws and the judges, against anyone, even their own masters.

8 Peasant status in Prussia

Statute from Frederick's *Code of Law*; published posthumously 1794

(In *Code général pour les états prussiens* Vol II (year ix), Paris, pp. 308–9)

Whoever belongs to the peasant class cannot without the permission of the State follow a bourgeois profession or destine his children to this profession. Every peasant is obliged to cultivate his land, in accordance with the principles of rural economy, in such a way as to meet the needs of the community. The State can therefore compel him to do so, if necessary by force.

What do you see as the essential elements in Frederick's policy regarding the peasants?

His approval in principle of the abolition of serfdom on humanitarian grounds and his ultimate commitment to standardizing peasant conditions in Prussia do seem to be genuine. However, his immediate concern in protecting the peasants was to bolster them as grain-producers, tax-payers and army recruits. A class of starving, exploited malcontents was of no use to the army or to the treasury; physical fitness and material prosperity were indispensable. Frederick therefore preserved land occupied by peasants from oversettlement or enclosure by the landlords (a process taking place unhindered elsewhere in Germany and in Britain). He also strove to ensure for them impartial justice in the courts (see section 4) and to protect them from excessive exploitation by their landlords by fixing three days a week as the maximum period of compulsory labour. He enforced this ruling on his own crown estates (which covered roughly one quarter of Prussia's territory and yielded one third of the public revenue), and conveyed plots of land to peasants as hereditary freehold, subject to the performance of the customary services and payment of dues, hoping that the nobles would follow his example. The forcefulness of his language in document 5 suggests that he expected opposition from the nobles. This was indeed the outcome, though it took the form of obstruction rather than outright opposition.

Frederick did not force the issue. In the last resort he was not prepared to provoke a confrontation or disturb the tacit understanding between himself and the nobility. His policy towards the peasants was paternalistic and gradualistic; it was certainly not radical and his hints at wider reform can be regarded as signposts for future action rather than policy for immediate implementation. Emancipation came only in 1807.

3 Reconstruction

Frederick's principal internal achievement—what he called his 'peaceful conquest' —was the 'Reconstruction' (*rétablissement*), Prussia's spectacular recovery and development in the two decades following the Seven Years War. Throughout the war, Prussia was repeatedly overrun from all sides and devastated: Pomerania and the New Mark by the Russians and Swedes, Halberstadt, Minden and Cleves by the French, Silesia by the Austrians; Berlin itself was twice occupied by the Russians, and East Prussia was temporarily annexed by Russia. In document 1, written in 1763 after a personal inspection of several provinces, Frederick draws a sombre picture of immediate post-war conditions.

Prussia after the Seven Years War

1   Frederick II on Reconstruction

Published *History of the Seven Years War;* 1763

('Histoire de la Guerre de Sept Ans', *Oeuvres de Frédéric le Grand* Vol V (1847), Berlin, pp. 232–3)

Prussia suffered most from this war. She was laid waste by Austrians, Frenchmen, Russians, Swedes and Germans . . .and spent one hundred and twenty five million thalers on maintaining her armies and on other military expenses. Pomerania, Silesia and the New Mark required large sums for their recovery. Other provinces, such as the Duchy of Crossen and the principalities of Halberstadt and Hohenstein, also needed heavy subsidies; and hard, sustained efforts were necessary to restore them to their pre-war condition, most of the fields being uncultivated for lack of seed and cattle, and there being a shortage of food of every kind for the civilian population. To relieve so much misery, 25 000 measures of wheat and flour, 17 000 measures of oats and 35 000 horses from the regiments and artillery were allocated among these provinces on an equitable basis; and food was distributed to nobles and peasants. In addition to these relief measures, the King contributed 3 000 000 thalers for the recovery of Silesia; 1 400 000 for Pomerania and the New Mark, 700 000 for the Electorate of Brandenburg and 100 000 for the Duchy of Cleves, besides 800 000 allotted to East Prussia. The taxes from the Duchy of Crossen and from Hohenstein and Halberstadt were reduced by one half. At length the people plucked up sufficient courage not to despair of their plight, to get down to work, and to make good by their energy and their industry the losses suffered by the State. . . Time, which cures and effaces all ills, will doubtless restore Prussia to her former abundance, prosperity and splendour.

2   Frederick II on Reconstruction

Letter from Frederick II to Electress Maria Antonia of Saxony; 9 April 1767

(*Oeuvres de Frédéric le Grand* Vol XXIV (1854), Berlin, p. 133)

Your Royal Highness will perhaps be curious to know what we are doing here. Well, Madam, we are producing children, we are constantly giving birth and preparing for baptisms. This is very much the order of the day, for after that horrible massacre of the human race [the Seven Years War], our most sacred duty is to make good the damage. If everyone were of the same opinion, Europe would long remain peaceful.

Agriculture, land reclamation and resettlement

Figure 9   Johann Christoph Frisch, *Frederick the Great Inspecting a Colonization Project*, 1777, oil on canvas, 45.7 × 62.2 cm (18 × 24½ ins), Marburg, Bildarchiv Foto Marburg. 'Suppose we establish 400 families this year. Next year we must settle 600, the year after 800, then 1200, and so forth. In twenty years time, that will make a fine number. Well, sir, why do you stare? Oh, I know what you think. You think: "There is an extravagant old man, who counts on living till the end of the century". Well, let me tell you I do not expect to live another two years. But in my situation, one must act as if one will never die' (Frederick the Great).

3   *Frederick II on Reconstruction*

Letter from Frederick II to Voltaire; 24 October 1773

(T. Besterman (ed) *Voltaire's Correspondence* Vol LXXXVI (1963), Geneva, p. 70)

It is over a month since I returned from my travels. I went to [West] Prussia★ to abolish serfdom, to reform some barbarous laws and promulgate some rational ones, to open a canal [the Bromberg canal] joining the Vistula, Netze, Warthe, Oder and Elbe, to rebuild some towns destroyed after the plague of 1709, to reclaim twenty miles of marshland and establish some degree of civilization in a region where the very name of civilization was unknown. From there I went to Silesia, to console my poor Jesuits for the severity of the court of Rome,† to confirm my support for their order, to organize a body of them in various provinces, where I protect them and make them useful to the country by their management of schools for the education of the young, to which they will devote themselves exclusively. In addition, I arranged for the building of sixty villages in Upper Silesia, where there was nothing but uncultivated land; each village contains twenty families. I had roads made in the mountains to facilitate trade, and rebuilt two towns which burned down; they were made of wood, and will be rebuilt in brick and even with cut stones quarried in the mountains. I shall not mention troops to you; that subject is too taboo at Ferney★★ for me to touch on it.

★ Annexed from Poland in the Partition of 1772
† Pope Clement XIV abolished the Society of Jesus in July 1773. It was not revived until 1814. (See section 5 documents 8 and 9)
★★ Voltaire's estate

4 Frederick II on Reconstruction

Letter from Frederick II to Voltaire; 5 December 1775

(T. Besterman (ed) *Voltaire's Correspondence* Vol XCII (1964), Geneva, p. 150)

There are no true riches except those which the earth produces. To improve your territory, to bring land under cultivation, to drain marshes, is to triumph over barbarism and to provide a livelihood for settlers of marriageable age, ready and willing to work at perpetuating the species and increasing the number of working citizens. Here we have imitated the agricultural methods of the English, which are very successful, and we have increased our cattle by a third. Their plough and seed-drill have not had the same success, the plough partly because our soil is too light, the seed-drill because it is too expensive for the common people and peasants. On the other hand, we have managed to grow rhubarb in our gardens. It retains all the qualities of and is identical to the kind imported from the East. This year we have produced ten million pounds of silk and we have increased our beehives by one third.

5 Frederick II on Reconstruction

Letter from Frederick II to Voltaire; 10 January 1776

(T. Besterman (ed) *Voltaire's Correspondence* Vol XCIII (1964), Geneva, p. 16)

I must say that, apart from Libya, few states can boast of having as much sand as we do. However, this year we are reclaiming seventy-six thousand acres of land; this land will support seven thousand cows; their manure will fertilize and improve our sand, and the harvests will be better. I know that men cannot change the nature of things; but I think that by dint of hard work and application one can succeed in improving a barren terrain and making moderately good land of it; and that is something to be getting on with.

6 Frederick II on Reconstruction

Article by De Launay (see p. 39); 1789

(De Launay, 'Justification du système d'économie politique et financière de Frédéric II', quoted in *Oeuvres de Frédéric le Grand* Vol XXIV (1854), Berlin, p. 323)

On his return from the war [of the Bavarian Succession 1778–9] and on the very day of his arrival, he summoned me. I found him still covered with dust, but already busy with the needs of his people. He asked Minister of State Michaelis why there was so much uncultivated land in the region bordering Saxony, which he had just crossed, and hearing that these lands belonged to poor landowners and to communities without the means to exploit them, he replied: 'And why was I not told? Understand that when in my State there are things which are beyond the capacity of my subjects, it is for me to provide for them, and for them to gather the fruits. I assign to you three hundred thousand thalers to have these lands brought under cultivation; you will tell me if that is insufficient.'

7 Frederick II on Reconstruction

23 July 1779

(Adapted from B. H. Latrobe (ed) *Characteristic Anecdotes and Miscellaneous Authentic Papers of Frederick II* (1788), London, pp. 180–1, 192–3)

Frederick Ranger! Why are these sand-lands* uncultivated?

Ranger Brandt They do not belong to the royal forests; they are part of the open country. Corn is sown on some of them. On our right hand, firs have been planted.

Frederick Who planted the firs?

* Land under reclamation some thirty miles north of Berlin. The account is by a local official, Fromme, who accompanied Frederick on his visit to this area.

Ranger Brandt   Your Majesty's Farmer-General, who is here.

Frederick (to Fromme)   Well, tell my Privy-Councillor Michaelis that it is my pleasure that the sand-land be cultivated. (*To the Ranger*) But do you know how firs are planted?

Ranger Brandt   Oh, yes, Sire.

Frederick   Well, how are they planted: from west to east, or east to west?

Ranger Brandt   From west to east.

Frederick   Right; but do you know why?

Ranger Brandt   Because we have strong winds mainly from the west.

Frederick   You are right . . . (To Fromme) Your subjects seem to be in very good circumstances.

Fromme   Yes, Sire. I can prove by the provincial registries that they are worth a capital of 50 000 thalers.

Frederick   I like that.

Fromme   Eleven years ago, a peasant died who had 11 000 thalers in the provincial bank.

Frederick   You must take care to keep them in these good circumstances.

Fromme   It is certainly good that the subjects are rich; but it makes them indolent, as is the case here. They have complained of me to your Majesty seven different times, in order to get rid of their [feudal] services.

Frederick   I dare say they had reason to do so.

Fromme   I humbly beg your Majesty's pardon. The matter has been enquired into, and it has been found in every case that far from having oppressed the subjects, I had merely required from them what it was their duty to do. But the affair rested there. The peasants are never punished: your Majesty always supposes them to be in the right.

Figure 10   Adolf von Menzel (1815–1905), *Frederick the Great on Inspection Tour* (a nineteenth-century reconstruction).

Frederick   The devil! These people will be wanting money from me, I suppose?

Fromme   Oh no, your majesty! They are full of joy that you have been graciously pleased to visit the district!

Frederick   They'll get nothing out of me, though.

Berlin, Staatsbibliothek Preussischer Kulturbesitz, Bildarchiv.

36

Consult your notes on television programme 6 'The Château and the Cottage'. What do documents 3–7 suggest about Frederick's tours of inspection compared with the activities of the French court?

Specimen answer

Frederick's tours of inspection were no mere ceremonial processions in the manner of Louis XIV or Louis XV. Frederick was actively involved in directing the Reconstruction and checking, by on-the-spot investigation and interviewing the locals, that his 'cabinet orders' were carried out. Contrast his first-hand and up-to-date knowledge (e.g. fertilization, afforestation) with the escapism of the French court into the peasant arcadia of *le petit hameau* at Versailles.

Discussion

For Frederick, one of the greatest achievements of Reconstruction was land reclamation and resettlement. 'The first object in any state is to increase its population in proportion as the land is capable of feeding its inhabitants' (section 8 document 7). This was traditional policy since the Great Elector, but Frederick applied it far more intensively than his predecessors. Particularly impressive was the reclamation of marshland along the rivers Oder, Warthe and Netze (including territory annexed from Poland in 1772). Altogether some 300 000 immigrants, mainly non-Prussian Germans, were resettled and some 900 new villages were established. By 1786 one in every five of the population was of immigrant origin. As a result of resettlement and (principally) annexations, Frederick doubled Prussia's population. Note Riesbeck's comments:

> No prince can manifest more regard for mankind than what is shown by the king of Prussia every day. He interests himself as much in the welfare of a common farmer as in the flourishing of the greatest house of trade in his dominions. It is his greatest pride and his greatest pleasure to read in the yearly lists that the population of his country has increased. He has not been seen so cheerful for many years as he was upon finding, by the list given in last year, that the number of the new-born children within the year far surpassed the number of the dead. *A king who has this way of thinking is a warrior only when necessity compels him to it.*
>
> *Travels through Germany, translated by Mr Maty* Vol III (1787), London, p. 9 (my italics)

Taxation

8 *Frederick II on thrift*

Published essay; 1777

('Essai sur les formes du gouvernement et sur les devoirs des souverains', *Oeuvres de Frédéric le Grand* Vol IX (1848), Berlin, pp. 204–7)

No government can do without taxes. . . The ruler responsible for all the public needs must have enough to live on; the judges must be paid, to keep them from sharp practice; the soldier must be maintained, so that he commits no act of violence for lack of money to live on; similarly those in charge of finances must be adequately paid so that necessity does not oblige them to maladminister the public funds. These various expenses demand considerable sums. In addition, there are the funds laid aside each year for emergencies. All this, however, must necessarily be levied on the people. The great art lies in raising these funds without oppressing the citizens. In order that the taxes shall be equitable and not arbitrary, censuses are taken, which, if they are accurately carried out, make the expenses proportionate to the capacity of the individual. So vital is this that it would be an unpardonable error if the taxes, through being clumsily imposed, discouraged the farmer from his work; after paying tax he and his family must still be able to live with a certain affluence. These 'foster-fathers' of the State, far from being oppressed, must be encouraged to cultivate their land thoroughly; for it is here that the country's true riches lie. The land furnishes the most basic foodstuffs, and those who work it are, as we have said, the true foster-fathers of society. . . Another kind of tax, levied on the towns, is the Excise. This requires to be carefully arranged, so as not to tax the most basic necessities of life, such as bread, small-beer, meat, etc, which would affect soldiers, workers and craftsmen; this would be to the people's detriment in that labour costs would increase and consequently our goods would become so expensive that we would lose the foreign credit for them. . .

Finally we must mention the best ways of ensuring a constant and abundant supply of the provisions that are indispensable if the kingdom is to remain prosperous. The first task is to pay close attention to agriculture, to cultivate all land capable of producing, to increase cattle in order to raise the supply of milk, cheese and manure; next, to keep accurate records of the number of bushels of the various kinds of grain yielded in good, average and bad years, to deduct from that the amount consumed, and, from the result, to discover the amount of surplus produce that can be exported or the shortfall for domestic consumption, to be made up. Every ruler concerned with the public welfare should provide granaries abundantly stocked, in order to supplement poor harvests and prevent famine. In Germany in the bad years 1771 and 1772 we saw the misfortunes suffered by Saxony and the provinces of the Empire, because this useful precaution had been neglected.

Exercise

Reconsider Frederick's attitude to the peasants in section 2 documents 4–8, in the light of documents 7–8.

Specimen answer

Possibly you found Frederick's conservative attitude unsympathetic. Note, however, his obvious concern for the wellbeing and prosperity of the peasants as producers of wealth, albeit within the existing social structure, and that his first priority was to ensure food supplies.

Complaints of Frederick's 'meanness' may be contrasted with the understanding of his deliberate thrift shown by Riesbeck:

> The taxes in the king of Prussia's dominions are subject to no alteration. In the very pressure of the Silesian war, when all Europe thought that the Prussian country must be drained to the uttermost farthing, they were not raised a sixpence; and had the war been longer and still more violent, they would not have been raised. This is due to the perfect knowledge which the king has of the state of the country, and his aversion to despotism and arbitrary power. He knew that taxes are doubly distressing to the farmers amid the desolations and distresses of war, and that any increase of them must be extremely pernicious, at a time when from the absence of the troops, the consumption of the produce is lessened, the country plundered by incursions of the enemy, and many useful hands taken from the plough.
>
> *Travels through Germany, translated by Mr Maty*, Vol II (1787), London, pp. 268–9

Industrial development and mercantilism

Frederick's policy of Reconstruction was actively interventionist: the economy was state-directed; there was no question of allowing the free play of market forces. In 1740 Prussia was an agrarian state, exporting, prior to 1763, a small amount of linen, grain and wool. While the mainstay of Reconstruction remained agricultural development, Frederick put enormous effort into creating and fostering industries. These were subsidized, regulated and coordinated by the state, which was, through the army, the largest single consumer. The principal industries were the manufacture of silk, woollens, paper, glass, iron, steel and porcelain. As well as supplying army requirements, however, Prussian industry was required to produce an export surplus, and was protected from foreign competition by high tariff barriers. With the annexation of Silesia, Prussia acquired an area rich in mineral resources; and in addition to the trade routes of the Oder, with the annexation of West Prussia she also controlled the Vistula. Considerable effort went into improving communications, particularly by the construction of canals. Though Frederick's efforts to sustain the porcelain and silk industries were less successful and his attempts to promote overseas trading companies were a failure, by 1786 Prussia came next after the three great producers of manufactured goods, England, France and Holland.

Frederick followed the mercantilist[7] policy laid down by his predecessors since the Great Elector—the direction, subsidizing, regulating and coordinating of industry, agriculture, trade and finance *by the State in the interests of the State*. There was nothing intrinsically original about his policy which, again, was guided by his perception of military priorities. The historians Marriot and Robertson write:

> Frederick had before his mind night and day the conduct and conditions of a big war. Prussia was poor; she had neither the financial machinery of an industrial state nor the assets on which to borrow; she must therefore, have reserves in men, money, food and equipment, in order to be self-sufficing. Necessity, as well as his own reasoned convictions, made him a narrow mercantilist... Wealth was so many barrels of thalers piled up in his treasury; tariffs, bounties, prohibitions must be freely used to encourage the growth of crops, the breeding of beasts, the development of those industries that would make Prussia absolutely independent of friend or foe.
>
> J. A. Marriot and C. G. Robertson *The Evolution of Prussia* (third edition 1968), Oxford University Press, p. 129.

Frederick's economic policy was criticized in his own day and has been since. Private manufacturers complained of unfair competition from the state enterprises, with their subsidies and monopolies. Peasants, burdened with feudal services, complained that the nobles were the beneficiaries of Frederick's grants to agriculture. All consumers complained of the Excise—Frederick's special indirect taxes on salt, sugar, coffee, tobacco, wine and beer—and there was a considerable amount of smuggling in these goods. Land reclamation and canal construction were resented by the peasants assigned to the work. Frederick's policy of hoarding capital in the treasury was criticized because the funds thus saved were withdrawn from general circulation. On the advice of the French *philosophe* Helvétius, Frederick in 1766 introduced a new system of collecting indirect taxes by the *Régie*, a special government department under a team of French tax-farmers headed by De Launay. The rigorous methods and high salaries of the customs officers (popularly known as 'coffee-sniffers') were particularly resented and the *Régie* was abolished immediately after Frederick's death. In document 11 Frederick defends his protectionist policy to De Launay and implicitly rejects the new principles of economics advocated by the Physiocrats and Adam Smith (see Units 25–27).

9 Frederick II on trade and industry

Letter from Frederick II to Voltaire, 5 September 1777

(T. Besterman (ed) *Voltaire's Correspondence* Vol XCVII (1964), Geneva, pp. 73–4)

I have returned from Silesia, and was very pleased with it. Agriculture there is making very marked progress; industry is prospering: we have exported five million thalers worth

[7] Mercantilism is discussed in Units 25–27 on Adam Smith's *The Wealth of Nations*.

Figure 11a *Silk Dyeing in Prussia*

Figure 11b *Tapestry Dyeing in Prussia*

Figure 11c *Glass Manufacture in Prussia*

These three engravings are by A. Barrati, 1779. Berlin, Archiv für Kunst und Geschichte. 'Man must labour, as the ox must pull the plough' (Frederick the Great).

of linen, and one million two hundred thousands worth of cloth. A cobalt mine has been discovered in the mountains, which can supply the whole of Silesia.* We are producing a vitriol as good as that made abroad. A most inventive man is developing an indigo identical to that of India; we can turn iron into steel in greater quantities and far more simply than by Réaumur's† process. Since 1756 (when the war began) our population has increased by a hundred and eighty thousand. In short, it is as if all the scourges which ruined this poor province had never been;** and I may tell you that I feel agreeably satisfied to see a province make such great progress. These tasks have by no means prevented me from scribbling down my ideas on paper; and to save the trouble of copying them by hand, I have had printed six copies of my reflections, of which I send you one.††

* Cobalt was used as a pigment in the manufacture of ceramics
† Réaumur was an eighteenth-century French scientist
** The War of the Austrian Succession and the Seven Years' War
†† Frederick's *Essay on the Forms of Government and on the Duties of Sovereigns*

10 Frederick II on trade and industry

Published essay; 1777

('Essai sur les formes du gouvernement et sur les devoirs des souverains', *Oeuvres de Frédéric le Grand* Vol IX (1848), Berlin, p. 206)

For a country to remain prosperous, it is absolutely essential for it to enjoy a favourable balance of trade: if it pays more for imports than it earns by exports, it must inevitably become poorer year by year . . . The ways to avoid this loss are: to manufacture at home all the raw material you possess, to process foreign materials in order to gain the skills and to produce them cheaply so as to obtain foreign credit. As for trade, that depends on three factors: the surplus products that you export, the products of your neighbours, whom you enrich by buying them, and on the foreign goods that you need and that you import.

11 Frederick II on free trade

Letter from Frederick II to De Launay

(In W. Hubatsch *Frederick the Great of Prussia. Absolutism and Administration* (1975), London, pp. 71–2)

Your intentions are good but you are ahead of your time. When the right moment comes I shall do as you advise, but to anticipate that time would ruin everything. You know my territories. The soil, for the most part, is sandy, dry and infertile. Grain production is too low to meet the whole population's needs, and the more fertile regions cannot completely supply those less favoured. Grazing lands are similarly insufficient. Cattle are small, scrawny and few in number, and my subjects are compelled to buy from Poland. As oil, spices, sugar, coffee and hundreds of other products have to be imported, they impose a considerable drain on the resources of the State. Were I to allow my subjects to import manufactured goods from abroad—which would please them very much—where would the process end? In all countries luxury tends to gain the upper hand. Soon all our foreign reserves—from our exports of wool, linens and wood—would be spent. Sheer necessity compels me to watch carefully our balance of payments and to open my hand not to give money to foreigners, but to receive from them. I prohibit imports as much as I can so that my subjects shall be encouraged to produce those things which I forbid them to get from elsewhere. Admittedly their early efforts are crude, but time and practice will bring perfection and we must show patience with first attempts.

4 The Rule of Law

Riesbeck (p. 38) referred to Frederick's 'aversion to despotism and arbitrary power'; and to describe Frederick's rule as 'absolute' or 'despotic' is held by some historians to be a misnomer, in that it suggests freedom from restraints and the right to act arbitrarily. Certainly, Frederick strongly deprecated the divine-right notion that the king was not accountable to any man-made law. He ordered that in the event of a clash between his executive directives and the law of the land as laid down by statute, his directives should be regarded as null and void. 'The ruler', he explained, 'is not a despot ruling merely according to his own whim' (section 1 document 5). This represents a significant departure in the concept of monarchy, away from the view of the monarch as a law unto himself (Frederick-William I had insisted that he was above the law) to what some historians have called 'absolutism with a conscience' and what the historian Peter Gay somewhat paradoxically terms 'constitutional absolutism'.

As the fountain of justice, the monarch traditionally took *ad hoc* decisions in legal cases. Frederick, by contrast, aimed at a fixed and systematized judicature within a framework of clearly defined laws, independent of royal interference. He directed the radical reform of the judicial system with the aim of making it speedy, cheap and available to all. He introduced a uniform, tiered system of courts, a trained, salaried and independent judiciary and, with the help of eminent jurists, the codification of Prussian law in the *Codex Fridericianus* of 1749. In its final revised form, published posthumously in 1794 as the *Allgemeines Landrecht*, Frederick's *General Code* (which lasted in essence until 1900) was 'one of the most important monuments of the Prussian Enlightenment' (Hubatsch 1973).

Codification

1 Frederick II on codification

Speech to the Academy of Sciences; 22 January 1750

('Dissertation sur les raisons d'établir ou d'abroger les lois', in *Oeuvres de Frédéric le Grand* Vol IX (1848), Berlin, pp. 24–5)

A perfect code of laws would be a masterpiece of human intelligence in the art of statesmanship. It would show a unity of design and rules so exact and so well-proportioned that a state governed according to these laws would be like a watch in which all the springs have been made for a single purpose. It would show a deep understanding of human psychology and national character. Punishments would be moderate, so that, while maintaining sound morals, they would be neither too lenient nor too severe. Clear and precise edicts would never give rise to litigation; they would consist of an exquisite selection of the best civil laws and in the adaptation, ingenious yet simple, of these laws to the nation's usage. Everything would be foreseen, everything would be coordinated and nothing would be subject to disadvantages; however, perfection is not humanity's lot.

The monarch and the law

2 Frederick II on the rule of law

Confidential memorandum intended for the use of his heir; 1768

('Testament politique' (1768) in G. B. Volz (ed) *Die Politischen Testamente Friedrichs des Grossen* (1920), Berlin, p. 111)

It is not at all proper for the monarch to interfere in the process of the law; the laws alone should rule and the monarch's duty is confined to protecting them. Security of goods and

Figure 12 Title page of the French version of *The Codex Fridericianus*, 1751. Reproduced by permission of the British Library Board. At Sans-Souci was a mill that Frederick sought to purchase and demolish. The miller refused every offer. Finally, Frederick's spokesman said 'Don't you realize that the King can take it by force if he wants to?' 'Is there then no Supreme Court at Berlin?' replied the miller. His answer was reported to Frederick. The mill still stands at Sans-Souci.

property is the basis of society and all good government. This law holds good for the monarch as for the meanest of his subjects; he must see that it is observed, and punish with the utmost rigour any judges who may contravene it.

3 Frederick II on justice

Letter from Frederick II to Voltaire; 13 August 1775

(T. Besterman (ed) *Voltaire's Correspondence* Vol XCI (1964), Geneva, pp. 160–1)

The protector of the Calas and Sirven family deserved to have the same success in the case of D'Etallonde.[8] You have had the rare advantage of reforming, from your retreat, the cruel sentences passed by the judges in your country, and to make those blush who, placed close to the throne, should have anticipated you. For myself, I confine myself in my own country to preventing the powerful from oppressing the poor, and to mitigating sentences which occasionally strike me as too severe. That is one part of my work. When I tour the provinces, everyone comes to me; I investigate all complaints, either personally or through others, and I make myself useful to persons of whose existence I was unaware before I received their petitions. This inspection makes the judges more attentive and prevents trials from being too harsh and rigorous.

4 Frederick II on justice

Published essay; 1777

('Essai sur les formes du gouvernement et sur les devoirs des souverains', *Oeuvres de Frédéric le Grand* Vol IX (1848), Berlin, p. 201)

The laws, if they are good, must be clearly expressed, so that they cannot be exploited

---

[8] see section 5 document 10

by sharp practice, their spirit evaded and the fate of individuals decided arbitrarily and unsystematically. Procedure must be as short as possible, in order to prevent the ruin of the parties, who would otherwise spend in unnecessary costs what is due to them in justice and by good right. This branch of administration cannot be too closely supervised, so that every possible obstacle may be put in the way of the greed of judges and the boundless self-interest of lawyers. Everyone is to be kept to his duties by periodical visits to the provinces, where anyone who thinks himself wronged can venture to bring his complaints before the commission of enquiry; and those found guilty of sharp practice must be severely punished. It is perhaps superfluous to add that the punishment must never exceed the crime; that arbitrary force must never be applied in place of the law; and that it is better for a monarch to be too indulgent than too severe.

5 *Frederick II on equality before the law*

Cabinet order from Frederick II to Baron Von Zedlitz★; 7 November 1777

(R. Stadelmann *Preussens Könige in ihrer Thätigkeit für die Landescultur, Part II: Friedrich der Grosse* (1882), Leipzig, p. 487)

I am very displeased to learn that poor people involved in lawsuits in Berlin are treated harshly and are threatened with arrest or actually arrested, as happened to Jacob Dreher at the hands of the Leibemühl Department in East Prussia, where he was staying in connection with a trial, and the police sought to arrest him. Although I have already strictly forbidden this sort of thing, I must nevertheless hereby inform you (and in particular Minister of State von Münchhausen†) that in my eyes a poor peasant is as worthy as the most distinguished count and the richest nobleman, and the law exists for high and low alike. I must therefore most earnestly request that poor people shall not be subjected to such harsh and arbitrary treatment and even threatened with imprisonment prior to routine cases. Rather they are to be given a sympathetic hearing and their lawsuits should be completed all the sooner, so that they may be allowed to go about their business and have no need to delay so long. You will therefore act accordingly in future.

★ Minister of Justice
† Formerly president of the Supreme Court, at this time responsible for the administration of justice in Silesia

The case of Miller Arnold

Frederick's role in the case of the Miller Arnold (1779) was as celebrated in contemporary Europe as Voltaire's in the Calas case. Arnold, a miller from the New Mark, claimed that he had been wrongfully dispossessed of his land through inability to pay his rent, as a result of the unlawful diversion of water from his mill by a local official. The case eventually came before the Supreme Court at Berlin which, confirming the ruling of the local appeal court at Küstrin, dismissed it. Arnold petitioned Frederick, who intervened in person and found in Arnold's favour (almost certainly without justification, though with the best intentions), suspecting the courts of class prejudice. He had several Supreme Court judges gaoled for nine months and dismissed the Minister of Justice. His admirers hailed the case as an example of 'enlightened absolutism' overriding vested interests.

6 *Frederick II on the case of Miller Arnold*

Cabinet order to all law courts; 12 December 1779

(B. H. Latrobe (ed) *Characteristic Anecdotes and Miscellaneous Authentic Papers of Frederick II* (1788) London, p. 285)

This is an act of the most flagrant injustice, and directly contrary to the gracious will of his Majesty, who means to be a father to his country. It is his Majesty's express will that throughout his dominions justice shall be impartially administered to every one of his subjects, whether they be noble or non-noble, whether they be rich or poor, without respect of persons. His Majesty is therefore determined severely to punish those judges who have decided in the case of the Miller Arnold, and to hold them out to all his courts as a dreadful instance of the consequence of neglected or perverted justice; and his Majesty would have them to know that the meanest peasant, nay even the beggar, is equally with his Majesty entitled to the rights of humanity, and has an equal claim upon strict and impartial justice.

Exercise

'It is not at all proper for the monarch to interfere in the process of the law' (Frederick, document 2). Was not Frederick's role in the case of Miller Arnold a denial of the 'rule of law' by his own definition?

Discussion

Scholars still argue about the case; but it seems that as the courts decided at the time, Arnold was a vexatious litigant and Frederick's intervention was precipitate, high-handed and arbitrary and seems to be an obvious violation of the rule of law.

It is arguable, however, that in his capacity as the supreme fountain of justice, Frederick was entitled under his own laws to reverse the decision of the Supreme Court—a prerogative he certainly retained in criminal cases. He saw his function as that of a sort of 'court of conscience' (see Units 4–5 section 2). Certainly, he believed that he exercised an overall supervisory jurisdiction: the ruler 'must punish with the utmost rigour any judges who may contravene the law'. Ritter sums up Frederick's attitude well: 'Frederick's interference, though mistaken, was not really a violation of his principles, but actually their indirect confirmation'.

Exercise

German historians point to Prussia as the model of a state where the rule of law was strictly observed. This view was shared by Riesbeck:

> The Prussian government is generally considered in other countries as the most despotic that exists, though in fact nothing can be less so. The maxim which is the foundation of the British constitution: *Rex in regno suo superiores habet Deum et Legem*[9], is nowhere so well observed as it is here. People will not surely call a rigid observation of the laws which promote the good of the state 'despotism'; and what instances are there of the king's ever having allowed himself anything that bespoke arbitrary sentiments? In no country are the rights of reason, the rights of nature, the customs and particular statutes which do not militate against the happiness of the whole, better observed and guarded than they are in the Prussian dominions. Nowhere does government direct all its steps so exactly according to the law as it does here.
>
> *Travels through Germany, translated by Mr Maty*, Vol II (1787), London, pp. 260–1

Do you agree?

Specimen answer

As the case of Miller Arnold makes clear, Frederick demanded the scrupulous observation of his subjects' legal rights and their protection from the arbitrary abuse of executive power by his officials. In this sense Prussia deserved the reputation of a state governed by the rule of law, which she enjoyed until 1933.

Discussion

Nevertheless, admirers of the British constitution, like Montesquieu (see Course Anthology Vol 1 pp. 131–4), Fielding or Gibbon (see Units 10–12 section 18), would

[9] 'The king in his realm is under the authority of God and the law' (dictum of the thirteenth-century English jurist, Bracton).

not agree with Riesbeck. They would argue that a basic corollary of the rule of law lies in some formal control of absolute power. In England, sovereignty resided in the king in Parliament: the king's will was circumscribed by law as laid down by Parliament and was subject in several important areas to the scrutiny and consent of representative institutions. In Prussia the opposite was the case: the former representative bodies of the nobility had been eliminated by the Great Elector and Frederick-William I. Frederick retained full executive and legislative power in his own hands, and used both to the full, taking his own unaided decisions, making a point of not seeking advice and fiercely resenting unsolicited opinions from his ministers. His renunciation of any desire to interfere with the due process of law, though wholly admirable, was a self-imposed restriction, not a result of any constitutional system of checks and balances. He kept the law because he chose to, not because he had to: like Gibbon's Antonine emperors who 'were pleased with considering themselves as the accountable ministers of the laws' (Course Anthology Vol 1, p. 245), 'the first servant of the state' was 'obliged to act . . . as if . . . he were accountable to his citizens' (section 1 document 3). In other words, Frederick however 'enlightened', remained 'absolute'; and Bracton's dictum, which is indeed 'the foundation of the British constitution', cannot properly be applied to Prussia.

Criminal justice

While deprecating royal interference with the process of civil justice as a denial of the rule of law and the independence of the courts, Frederick insisted on retaining his prerogative as supreme court of appeal in criminal cases. All cases of treason, forgery, murder, and all sentences of death, hard labour or corporal punishment were automatically forwarded to Frederick for his personal review.

On his accession Frederick abolished judicial torture for all but the most serious capital offences, and abolished it altogether in 1754. The traditional view is that he was inspired by the humanitarian ideas of his time. Doubts have been cast on this interpretation by an American scholar, J. H. Langbein, who argues that the abolition of torture as a means of extracting evidence owed nothing to Enlightenment influences, but resulted from important changes in the continental law of evidence, which reduced the importance hitherto attached to a personal confession of guilt by the accused in favour of careful evaluation of circumstantial evidence, and thereby rendered the use of torture unnecessary. These changes had come into being in the seventeenth century and by the time of Frederick-William I 'the new law of proof had already displaced judicial torture' (J. H. Langbein *Torture and the Law of Proof* (1977), Chicago University press, p. 61).

7   *Frederick II on torture*

Speech to the Academy of Sciences; 22 January 1750

('Dissertation sur les raisons d'établir ou d'abroger les lois', *Oeuvres de Frédéric le Grand* Vol IX (1848), Berlin, pp. 28–9)

Nothing is crueller than torture. The Romans tortured their slaves, whom they regarded as a kind of domestic chattel; but no citizen was ever put to the torture. In Germany,* criminals are tortured after conviction in order to make them confess their crimes with their own lips; in France, torture is used to discover evidence or to reveal accomplices. The English once had the ordeal by fire and water . . .

Pardon me, I must protest against torture; I make so bold as to take humanity's side against a practice shameful to Christians and civilized peoples, and, I would add, as cruel as it is useless.

Quintilian,† wisest and most eloquent of orators, says in his discussion of torture that it is a question of temperament. A robust villain will deny his guilt; an innocent weakling will confess himself guilty. A man is accused, evidence exists, the judge is uncertain, he wishes to clarify himself, the poor wretch is put to the torture. If he is innocent, how barbarous to make him suffer martyrdom! If, overwhelmed by pain, he is forced to give evidence against himself, what dreadful inhumanity to put to agonizing pain and to condemn to death a virtuous citizen against whom there are nothing but suspicions! It would be better to pardon twenty guilty men than to sacrifice one innocent one. If laws are to be laid down for the good of the people, should we tolerate such laws, which authorize judges to commit these outrages and which revolt humanity? In Prussia torture was abolished eight years ago; we are sure of never confusing innocent and guilty, and justice is done no less than before.

★ i.e. outside Prussia
† Roman writer on rhetoric

8 Frederick II on torture

Letter from Frederick II to Voltaire; c 20 August 1766

(T. Besterman (ed) *Voltaire's Correspondence* Vol LXII (1961), Geneva, pp. 130–1)

The recent cases of Calas and Sirven and lastly the events at Abbeville,★ make me suspect that justice is badly administered in France . . . I am sure that the law is badly in need of reform and that the courts should never be left the power to carry out death sentences without review by the superior courts and ratification by the monarch. It is a pitiful thing to quash convictions and sentences after the victims have perished;† . . . What disgusts me most is the barbarous custom of putting the condemned to torture before taking them to be executed. It is a gratuitous piece of cruelty, which horrifies sympathetic souls who still retain some sentiment of humanity . . .

★ The case of De La Barre; see section 5 document 10
† as in the Calas case

9 Frederick II commutes a death-sentence

Cabinet order from Frederick II to Baron Von Zedlitz;★ 23 April 1776

(B. H. Latrobe (ed) *Characteristic Anecdotes and Miscellaneous Authentic Papers of Frederick the Great* (1788), London, p. 40)

I have great objections in my own mind to signing the sentence of death pronounced by the court against the incendiary Döpel. Both he and his accomplice Weiss are said to be still very young; and on that account it is my pleasure that neither of them be executed, but that they be confined in the house of correction, and care be taken that during their confinement they be better instructed in their duty to society, and made sensible of the dreadful nature of their crime. You are therefore directed to have the warrant altered accordingly.

★ Minister of Justice

10 Frederick II on criminal justice

Letter from Frederick II to Voltaire; 11 October 1777

(T. Besterman (ed) *Voltaire's Correspondence* Vol XCVII (1964), Geneva, pp. 122–3)

No one can be arrested without my signature or punished unless I have ratified the sentence. Most of these delinquents are girls who have killed their children;★ there are few murders, and still fewer highway robberies. But as for those creatures who treat their offspring so cruelly, only those are executed whose act of murder we have been able to prove.

I have done what I can to prevent these unfortunate women from doing away with their offspring. Masters are obliged to report their maidservants if they become pregnant;

47

formerly these poor girls used to be forced to do public penance in church; I relieved them of this. In every province there are homes in which they can have their confinement and have their children brought up. Notwithstanding all these facilities, I have still not succeeded in ridding their minds of the unnatural prejudice that makes them do away with their children. At this very moment I am contemplating the abolition of the stigma formerly attaching to those who married unmarried mothers; I do not know whether I shall succeed. Perhaps I shall. As for torture, we abolished it entirely and it has not been used for over thirty years . . . We must follow the maxim that it is better to spare a guilty man than to punish an innocent one. After all, if we are uncertain of a man's innocence, is it not better to keep him under arrest than to execute him? Truth lies at the bottom of a well; it needs time to draw it up and it is often slow to appear; but we lose nothing by suspending judgement until we are absolutely clear about the facts and we can live with a quiet conscience, something with which every honest man must be concerned. Excuse this legal prattle. It is you who started me off on this topic; I would not have ventured to do so on my own. Matters of this sort form my daily duties; I have developed certain principles according to which I act, and I am simply setting them out for you.

* The traditional penalty for infanticide, based on Roman law, was for the guilty mother to be sewn in a sack and drowned. This was abolished by Frederick

11 Frederick II on criminal justice

Letter from Frederick II to Condorcet*; 24 October 1785

(*Oeuvres de Frédéric le Grand* Vol XXV (1854), Berlin, pp. 379–80

I turn to the subject of the laws, which Monsieur de Beccaria† has so well explained and on which you have written equally well. I am entirely of your opinion that the judges must not be in a hurry to pass sentence and that it is better to save a guilty man than to destroy an innocent one.

However I think experience has taught me that one must not overlook any of the reins with which we lead men, namely, rewards and punishments; and that there are cases where the atrocity of the crime must be punished with rigour. Murderers and arsonists, for example, deserve the death penalty, because they have assumed a tyrannical power over men's lives and possessions. I agree that a life sentence is indeed a crueller punishment than death; but it is not as striking as the punishment which takes place before the eyes of the crowd, because such spectacles make more impression than occasional talk about the pains suffered by those who languish in gaol.

I have done all in my power to reform justice in this country and to avoid abuses by the courts. The angels might succeed if they wished to take on the task; but having no connection with those gentlemen, we are reduced to relying on our fellow men, who are still very far from perfect.

* French *philosophe* and advocate of the idea of Progress
† Italian *philosophe*, author of *On Crimes and Punishments* (1764), a treatise on criminal law reform and one of the most influential works of the Enlightenment

Exercise

According to Langbein's thesis, resort to judicial torture had already diminished in practice before Frederick's accession. Does this suggest that Frederick's humanitarian arguments were merely 'window-dressing'?

Specimen answer

Not necessarily. Langbein's argument has no relevance to Frederick's reforms in other areas of criminal law, for example, his attitudes towards
1 the presumption of innocence and its importance, and
2 infanticide.

Discussion

No fewer than 100 articles of the *General Code* were devoted to the reform of the law on infanticide, which evidently caused much controversy in Prussia. The French military expert, Guibert, who visited Prussia in 1773, noted disapprovingly:

> The measures taken by his Prussian Majesty to promote the propagation of the species in his territories are not a little extraordinary. Pregnancy is rendered respectable, however it has been acquired: a big belly secures, by law, the licentious daughter from the reproaches of her parents, and a maidservant from the censure of her master and mistress, who are not suffered to turn her away or to ill-treat her or even to reprove her for what she has done.
>
> *Observations on the Military Establishment and Discipline of His Majesty the King of Prussia*, translated from the French by J. Johnson (1780), London. p. 47

Consider Frederick's attitude to marriages within the 'prohibited degrees' (section 5 document 6). Above all, note Frederick's strictures on capital punishment, his restriction of the number of capital offences to a mere handful and even then his reluctance to ratify death sentences. Statistics for the four years 1775 to 1778 show that Frederick signed an average of a dozen death-warrants a year; and that out of a total of forty-six only two were in respect of offences against property, as opposed to offences against the person. This represents a remarkable contrast to the incidence of capital punishment elsewhere in Europe, particularly in England where Parliament in the eighteenth century increased the number of capital offences from roughly fifty to over two hundred. Almost all the new offences were concerned with property. (See Units 4–5 section 1 on the role of the law, pp. 17–21.)

Contrast Frederick's conscientious review of all serious criminal cases with the position in England, where, despite the most liberal methods of trial, there was no automatic right of appeal against conviction or sentence until 1907 (*sic*).

Military discipline

Figure 13   Daniel Chodowiecki, *Discipline in the Prussian Army*, 1774, engraving—'Teach them to respect the stick' (Frederick the Great). Berlin, Archiv für Kunst und Geschichte.

Frederick's humanitarianism in civilian cases, however, may be contrasted with his deliberate retention of the institutionalized brutality of military discipline laid down for the rank and file by Frederick-William I, and characterized by floggings and the penalty of 'running the gauntlet' Dr J. Moore gives an account that is particularly striking, given the harsh standards of discipline in the British army of the time:

> The Prussian discipline on a general view is beautiful; in detail it is shocking ... In the park at Berlin, every morning may be seen the lieutenants of the different regiments exercising with the greatest assiduity, sometimes a single man, at other times three or four together; and now, if the young recruit show neglect or remissness, his attention is roused by the officer's cane, which is applied with augmenting energy, till he has acquired the full command of his firelock. He is taught steadiness under arms, and the immobility of a statue; he is informed that all his members are to move only at the word of command, and not at his own pleasure; that speaking, coughing, sneezing, are all unpardonable crimes; and when the poor lad is accomplished to their mind, they give him to understand that now it is perfectly known what he can do, and therefore the smallest deficiency will be punished with rigour. And although he should destine every moment of his time and all his attention to cleaning his arms, taking care of his clothes and practising the manual exercise, it is but barely possible for him to escape punishment ... However desirous a Prussian soldier may be to desert, the thing is almost impossible. The moment a man is missing, a certain number of cannons are fired, which announce the desertion to the whole country. The peasants have a considerable reward for seizing a deserter, and are liable to severe penalties if they harbour or aid him in making his escape and parties from the garrisons are sent after him in every direction. . .

Figure 14 Daniel Chodowiecki, *Running the Gauntlet*, 1774, engraving—'If my soldiers began to think, no one would remain in the ranks' (Frederick the Great). Berlin, Archiv für Kunst und Geschichte.

As to the common men, the leading idea of the Prussian discipline is to reduce them, in many respects, to the nature of machines; that they may have no volition of their own, but be actuated solely by that of their officers; that they may have such a superlative dread of those officers as annihilates all fear of the enemy;[10] and that they may move forwards when ordered, without deeper

[10] See Gibbon, 'it was an inflexible maxim of Roman discipline, that a good soldier should dread his officers far more than the enemy' (Course Anthology Vol I, p. 192).

50

reasoning or more concern that the flintlocks they carry along with them . . .
The king imagines . . . that discipline is the soul of an army; that men in the
different nations of Europe are, in those qualities which are thought necessary
for a soldier, nearly on a par; that in two armies of equal numbers, the degree
of discipline will determine how far one is superior to the other. The great
object therefore is to keep his own army at the highest possible degree of
perfection in this essential point. If that could be done by gentle means,
undoubtedly he would prefer it. He is not naturally of a cruel disposition.

A View of Society and Manners in France, Switzerland and Germany, Vol II
(1789), Dublin, pp. 101–13

5 Religion and Toleration

Ruling a predominantly Protestant state (90 per cent Lutheran, 3 per cent Calvinist, 7 per cent Catholic), Frederick was probably most admired by the French *philosophes* for his insistence on toleration of religious minorities. This certainly contrasted with the discrimination practised to a greater or lesser extent against Protestants in Catholic France and in Austria (under Maria Theresa) and, for that matter, against Catholics in Protestant Britain. What his admirers overlooked, however, was the fact that toleration was firmly established in Prussia under the Great Elector and Frederick-William I, both in the Rhineland provinces, where Catholics were in a majority, and in Prussia generally, as part of the policy of encouraging immigration. With the acquisition of mainly Catholic Silesia (1740) and West Prussia (1772) toleration became even more indispensable; it was also obviously essential in an army which included sizeable non-Protestant contingents. As for Frederick's own religious views, he much enjoyed speculation in the sceptical manner of Bayle, Voltaire and Hume.

Figure 15   Marble statues at Sans-Souci, of Apollo (left) and Venus (right), by F. G. Adam, 1740. 'All religions, when one examines them, are based on a system of more or less absurd myths' (Frederick the Great). Photographs by Paul Kafno.

1   Frederick II on religion

Letter from Frederick II to Voltaire; 24 October 1766

(T. Besterman (ed) *Voltaire's Correspondence* Vol LXIII (1961), Geneva, pp.38–9)

I congratulate you on the good opinion you have of humanity. For myself, who am very familiar with that 'two-legged featherless species',* because of the duties of my office, I

* A favourite expression of Voltaire's (see *Candide*, p. 27, 'a creature without wings but with two legs and a soul')

52

predict that neither you nor all the *philosophes* in the world will wean mankind from the superstition to which it clings . . .. Nevertheless, I do believe that the voice of reason, by raising itself against fanaticism, could render the future race more tolerant than it is in our day; and that would be a considerable advance.

2 Frederick II on religion

Letter from Frederick II to Voltaire; *c* 15 December 1766

(T. Besterman (ed) *Voltaire's Correspondence* Vol LXIII (1961), Geneva, p.188)

You suppose that I think that the people needs the curb of religion in order to be controlled; I assure you these are not my sentiments. On the contrary, my experience places me entirely on the side of Bayle:* a society could not exist without laws, but it could certainly exist without religion, provided that there is a power, which by punitive sanctions can compel the masses to obey these laws. This is confirmed by the experiences of the savages discovered on the Marianne Islands,† who had not a metaphysical idea in their heads. It is proved still more by the government of China, where theism is the religion of all the leading men in the state. However, as you see that in that vast kingdom the common people have abandoned themselves to the Buddhist superstition, I maintain that the same thing would happen elsewhere, and that a state purged of all superstition would not remain long in its purity but that new absurdities would take the place of the old ones, and within a short time, at that.

The little dose of good sense spread across the surface of the globe is, I think, sufficient to found a world-wide society, rather like that of the Jesuits, but not a state. I see the present work of the *philosophes* as very useful, because men ought to be made to feel ashamed of fanaticism and intolerance and because it is a service to humanity to fight these cruel and atrocious follies which turned our ancestors into ravening beasts. To destroy fanaticism is to dry up the most deadly source of division and hatred in European memory, the bloody traces of which are found among all its peoples.

* in *Miscellaneous Thoughts on the Comet of 1680*
† The Maldive Islands

3 Voltaire on Christianity

Letter from Voltaire to Frederick II; January 1767

(T. Besterman (ed) *Voltaire's Correspondence* Vol XLIV (1961), Geneva, p.19)

You are absolutely right, Sire: a courageous and wise ruler, with money, troops, laws, may rule men very well without the aid of religion, which is only designed to deceive them; but the stupid masses will soon invent one for themselves; and as long as there are knaves and fools, there will be religions. Ours is without doubt the most ridiculous, absurd and bloody that has ever infected the world. Your Majesty will do mankind an everlasting service by destroying this infamous superstition—I do not mean among the riffraff, who do not deserve to be enlightened and who require every kind of control—I mean among honest, thinking men, men who wish to reason. There are many of them; it is up to you to support them: charity begins in the home. My only pain at dying is in my deep regret at not helping you in this noble task, the finest and most worthy that the human mind can aspire to.

4 Frederick II on natural religion

Letter from Frederick II to d'Alembert; 18 October 1770

(*Oeuvres de Frédéric le Grand* Vol XXIV (1854), Berlin, p. 505)

Let me tell you that our religions of today resemble the religion of Christ as little as they resemble that of the Iroquois. Jesus was a Jew, and we burn the Jews;* Jesus preached tolerance, and we persecute; Jesus preached morality, and we fail to practise it; Jesus did not establish any dogma, and the Councils laid down a store of them. . . Jesus was in

* See *Candide*, p. 36

fact an Essene,† he was imbued with the morality of the Essenes, which is very similar to that of Zeno.** His religion was a pure deism, and see how we have embroidered it.

† Ascetic Jewish sect of the time of Christ
** The founder of Stoicism

5   Frederick II on tolerance

Published essay; 1777

('Essai sur les formes du gouvernement et sur les devoirs des souverains', *Oeuvres de Frédéric le Grand* Vol IX (1848), Berlin, pp.207–8)

There are few countries where the citizens share the same views on religion; often they differ completely, and some of them form different sects. The question therefore arises: must all citizens think alike, or can everyone be allowed to think as he wishes? Firstly, there are gloomy political thinkers who will tell you: 'Everyone must be of the same opinion, so that nothing may divide the citizens.' The theologian adds: 'Whoever does not share my beliefs is damned; . . . so we must burn them in this world so that they may be better off in the next'. Our answer to that is that no society will ever share the same beliefs; that most Christian nations are anthropomorphite and that most Catholics are idolatrous; for I shall never be persuaded that a peasant can distinguish between *latria* and *hyperdulia*:* he genuinely worships the image that he invokes. So there are a variety of heretics in all the Christian sects. Moreover, each believes whatever seems plausible to it. One can force some poor wretch to pronounce a certain formula, from which he witholds his inner consent; so that the persecutor has gained nothing. But if we go back to the origin of society, it is perfectly clear that the monarch has no right to dictate the citizen's beliefs.

One would surely have to be mad to imagine that some men said to one of their fellows: 'We raise you above us, because we wish to be slaves, and we give you authority to dictate our thoughts as you wish'. On the contrary, they said: 'We need you to maintain the laws that we wish to obey, to rule us wisely and to protect us; for the rest, we ask you to respect our liberty'. Such is the sentence that has been pronounced, and there is no appeal against it. Moreover, this very tolerance is so beneficial to the societies where it is established, that it constitutes the happiness of the State. Whenever there is freedom of religion, everyone lives peacefully; while persecution has given rise to the bloodiest, longest and most destructive civil wars. The least of the evils brought by persecution is that it compels its victims to emigrate: France has had whole provinces where the population has declined and which still feel the effects of the revocation of the Edict of Nantes.†

* The distinct categories of worship: a   to God; b   to the Virgin Mary
† The revocation of the Edict of Nantes (1598) by Louis XIV in 1685 ended the toleration extended to the French Huguenots (Protestants). Many Huguenot refugees settled in Prussia.

Exercise

What do documents 1–5 suggest of Frederick's religious beliefs?

Specimen answer

Though brought up a Lutheran, Frederick is obviously not a conventional Christian, or apparently a Christian at all. His views seem to mirror those of the Deists (see Gibbon, Units 10–12 section 10), believers in 'Natural Religion', a system of universal ethics, holding to belief in the existence of a 'Supreme Being', but not in the need for revelation. The ethical teachings of Jesus, as opposed to organized Christianity, he classifies as 'a pure deism'. He considers all conventional religions to be 'based on a system of more or less absurd myths'. Frederick regards metaphysics, speculation into the nature of God, as futile, the source of interdenominational squabbles and 'the most deadly source of division and hatred in European memory'; and here he probably had in mind the horrors of Catholic-Protestant bloodshed in the Thirty Years War (1618–48) which left Prussia prostrate. Frederick rejects Voltaire's suggestion that conventional religion is necessary to keep the masses in order; it is a matter of private conscience. Stoicism, as expounded in Cicero's *De Officiis* (*On Duties*) (which Frederick described as 'the best work on morals that has been or can be written'; compare Units 8–9, *Hume's Enquiry Concerning the Principles of Morals*, p. 39) and the *Meditations* of Marcus Aurelius, seems to be a particularly attractive form of Natural Religion for Frederick, with its ethos of right reason, duty and *humanitas* together with the Roman tradition of religious tolerance.

Church and State

Frederick's policy of toleration did not mean leaving the churches free to manage their own affairs. On the contrary, the organization of church affairs was closely supervised by the State through a special Department of Religion. Protestantism remained the official faith and, as head of the Lutheran church, Frederick was active in the appointment of bishops, giving preference to ecumenically minded candidates who would encourage interdenominational cooperation. The Catholic church required particularly careful handling, with its papal and (in Silesia) Austrian loyalties; again Frederick strove to influence appointments (though he had to do so indirectly), and to foster the loyalty of his Catholic subjects by such acts as the establishment of the Catholic Cathedral of St Hedwig in Berlin (consecrated in 1773). At the same time, however, he ordered that public prayers for the health of the Holy Roman Emperor should be discontinued. The clergy were entrusted with the task of running primary education: Frederick saw them as invaluable instruments for imparting the Prussian ethos of hard work, thrift and obedience.

Frederick's policy towards the Jews did not in fact go far beyond bare toleration; but this in itself was most welcome in Silesia, for example, where Maria Theresa's policy had been one of outright persecution. There was no question of equality of rights, however. The Jews of Prussia remained, as they had since the Great Elector, a tiny minority, confined to a separate and subordinate legal status, subject to varying degrees of discriminatory regulations as 'protected Jews' (*Schutzjuden*) and to a catalogue of special and onerous taxes. These regulations, revised by Frederick in 1753, aimed at permitting the activities of a small number of wealthy Jews as manufacturers (particularly in the silk industry) and bankers, while limiting the growth of a Jewish community. Though Frederick's officials urged him to liberalize the regulations in the interests of the economy, he actually increased their severity. 'I have never persecuted members of this sect, or anyone else', he declared in 1768, 'but I think it prudent to see that their numbers do not grow too great.'

6 *Frederick II on church and State*

Confidential memorandum intended for the use of his heir; 1752

('Political testament' (1752) in G. B. Volz (ed) *Die Politischen Testamente Friedrichs des Grossen* (1920), Berlin, pp. 31–2)

Catholics, Lutherans, Protestants, Jews and numerous other Christian [*sic*] sects live peacefully in this State. If the monarch, inspired by misplaced zeal, thought fit to declare himself for one of these religions, we would immediately see factions form, disputes develop, persecutions gradually begin and finally the persecuted religion leave its own country and thousands of subjects enrich our neighbours by their numbers and industry.

It is politically quite immaterial whether a monarch has a religion or has no religion. All religions, when one examines them, are based on a system of more or less absurd myths. It is impossible for a man of good sense who examines these matters not to see their error; but these prejudices, these errors, this element of the miraculous, is made for man, and one must show the people enough respect not to scandalize it in its religious beliefs, whatever they may be...

I am in a certain sense the 'pope' of the Lutherans and head of the Protestant church. I appoint the clergy, and require of them only morality and mildness. I decide marriage suits and am very indulgent in this respect, because basically marriage is only a civil contract which can be dissolved whenever both parties consent. Apart from brother and sister, mother and son, and father and daughter, I readily allow people to marry whom they please; for there is no harm in this sort of marriage.

The other Christian sects are all tolerated here; we silence the first man who seeks to ignite civil unrest and we treat the opinions of innovators with the ridicule they deserve. I am neutral between Rome and Geneva.* If Rome seeks to encroach on Geneva, Rome gets the worst of it; if Geneva seeks to oppress Rome, Geneva is condemned. In this way I can lessen religious hatreds by preaching moderation to all parties, and I try to unite them by reminding them that they are all fellow citizens, and that one can like a man who wears a red costume as much as another who wears a grey one.† I try to maintain friendly relations with the Pope, in order to win over the Catholics and make them understand that the policy of rulers is the same, even though their nominal religion is different. However, I advise my successors not to trust the Catholic clergy without solid proofs of its loyalty . . .

Most of the Catholics are in Silesia. We allow them the free exercise of their religion; but to prevent the monasteries from stifling in celibacy the hopes of their families, it is forbidden to become a monk or nun before the age of majority. In other respects, I allow the clergy every liberty and the rights proper to them. The parish priests are quite reliable people; the monks are more inclined to support the House of Austria. For this reason, I make them pay thirty per cent of their revenues to the State, so that they may be of some use.** The Jesuits of Silesia, the most dangerous of all the monks of that communion, are extremely fanatical for the House of Austria. To set one group off against another, I have invited educated French Jesuits to come to raise educational standards among the Silesian nobility, and thanks to the animosity that prevails between these French and German monks, I prevent them from conspiring together in favour of the house of Austria, which they might otherwise do.

* Echoes the line in Voltaire's *Henriade* (1728): '*je ne décide point entre Genève et Rome.*'
† i.e. the Catholic and Calvinist clergy
** The monasteries in Austria were exempt from taxation.

7 Frederick II on tolerance

Cabinet order to the Lutheran clergy; 18 January 1781

(B. H. Latrobe (ed) *Characteristic Anecdotes and Miscellaneous Authentic Papers of Frederick II* (1788), London, pp. 49–51)

His Majesty, from a thorough conviction that he thereby fulfils the duty of a good sovereign and father of his people, has laid down as an unalterable principle of his government, that every subject shall have liberty to believe whatever he can or will, and to serve God in whatever manner he likes, provided his principles of worship are not injurious to the peace of the State or subversive of morality. It is therefore his Majesty's will and pleasure that no constraint whatever in regard to the use or disuse of the new catechism and hymn-book shall be laid upon any of the churches, but everyone is in this respect at liberty to think and to act as he pleases . . . As to the hymn-book, everyone is at liberty to sing: '*Nun ruhen alle Wälder*',* or any other foolish, stupid nonsense he chooses. But the clergy must never forget toleration, as I shall never suffer them to persecute anyone.

* Now all the woodlands rest', a traditional Lutheran hymn, well known in its English version 'The duteous day now closeth'.

8 Frederick II on the Jesuits

Letter from Frederick II to Voltaire; 5 May 1767

(T. Besterman (ed) *Voltaire's Correspondence* Vol LXV (1961), Geneva, pp. 206–7)

We have just made a fresh advance in Spain: the Jesuits have been expelled from that kingdom. Furthermore, the courts of Versailles, Vienna and Madrid have asked the Pope to suppress a considerable number of monasteries. It is said that the Holy Father will have to agree, furious though he is. What a revolutionary turn of events, not to be expected even in the next century! The axe is laid to the roots of the tree: on one hand, the *philosophes* rise up against the absurdities of a revered superstition; on the other, excessive spending compels rulers to take over the goods of those recluses, the tools and mouthpieces of fanaticism. This building, undermined at its foundations, will collapse; and the nations will record in their annals that Voltaire was the instigator of this revolution that took place in the human mind in the eighteenth century.

9 *Frederick II on the Jesuits*

Letter from Frederick II to Electress Maria Antonia of Saxony; 1 February 1768

(*Oeuvres de Frédéric le Grand* Vol XXIV (1854), Berlin, p. 149)

The Great Powers, to relieve their boredom, are making war on the poor Jesuits, who will soon be banished from half of Europe. What astonishes me in the conduct of these kings is that they follow the example of the Holy Office [The Inquisition] and sequester the spoils of the outlawed party, doubtless to console themselves for losing the latter. For all that I am a heretic, I take great care not to follow their example, and I shall leave the Order in peace, as long as they do not seek to interfere in secular matters or to assassinate me or my relatives. Circuses keep lions and tigers for animal fights; why should Jesuits not be tolerated likewise? The most sociable of animals ought to have dealings with all other animals; and it is possible to live with Jesuits, Buddhist priests, Imams, and Rabbis, without biting them or being bitten by them. . . The greatest folly of our species is that we make use of demons in order to persecute one another and make life bitter for each other.

Exercise

Explain Frederick's attitude to the Jesuits in view of the hostility to them normally shown by the *philosophes*.

Specimen answer

Frederick's attitude towards the Jesuits after the dissolution of their Order in 1773 (compare section 3 document 3) is a classic example of his pragmatism: the Jesuits were justly renowned for the excellence of their teaching-methods—Voltaire was one of their former pupils!—so, with the provision that they refrained from interfering in politics, Frederick welcomed them to Prussia. He also hoped that the influence of the French Jesuits would counteract the anti-Prussian sentiments of the monks in mainly Catholic (formerly Austrian) Silesia (see document 6). Frederick was evidently amused by the irony of a free-thinker extending tolerance to a Catholic order disbanded by the Pope!

The case of De la Barre

Frederick readily contributed to Voltaire's campaign for the rehabilitation of Calas (1762–5) (see radio programme 20, 'Voltaire and the Calas Affair') but his attitude to the case of De la Barre in 1766 was more critical. Two young nobles, De la Barre and D'Etallonde, were convicted by the *parlement* of Abbeville of blasphemy, in failing to remove their hats and singing ribald songs in the presence of a religious procession. They were condemned to death and sentence was confirmed by the Paris *parlement*, which noted that irreligion was prevalent and that Voltaire's antireligious *Philosophical Dictionary* (1764) had been found in De la Barre's possession. D'Etallonde fled abroad, and through Voltaire's intervention with Frederick, obtained a commission in the Prussian army. De la Barre, however, was put to death, his tongue excised and his body burnt at the stake.

10 Frederick II on the case of De la Barre

Letter from Frederick II to Voltaire; 13 August 1766

(T. Besterman (ed) *Voltaire's Correspondence* Vol LXII (1961), Geneva, pp. 113–5)

I think you will already have received my reply to your last letter but one. I cannot find the execution at Abbeville as terrible as the unjust execution of Calas. Calas was innocent; he was the victim of fanaticism, and nothing in that terrible deed can excuse the judges. Far from it, they ignored the formal procedures and sentenced him to death without evidence, exhibits or witnesses.

The recent event at Abbeville is of a quite different nature. You will not dispute that every citizen must obey the laws of his country. Well, there are penalties laid down by the legislators for those who disturb the religion adopted by the nation. Discretion, decency, above all the respect that every citizen owes to the laws, oblige him not to insult the accepted religion and to avoid scandal and insolence. These are indeed bloody laws, which ought to be reformed by making the punishment proportionate to the crime; but as long as these rigorous laws remain the law of the land, the judges are bound to follow them. The religious party in France rails against the *philosophes* and accuses them of being the cause of all the evils that take place. During the last war, there were some madmen who claimed that the *Encyclopédie* was the cause of the misfortune suffered by the French armies . . .

. . . I offer refuge to the *philosophes*, provided that they behave themselves, and that they are as peaceful as the fine title that they possess implies; for all the truths that they proclaim are not worth peace of mind, the only benefit that men can enjoy on his 'atom' that they inhabit. As for myself, being in favour of reason without enthusiasm, I should like men to be reasonable and, above all, peaceful. We know the crimes inspired by religious fanaticism. Let us beware of introducing such fanaticism into philosophy, whose character should be mildness and moderation. Philosophy should pity the tragic end of a young man who committed an act of folly; it should point out the excessive harshness of a law made in crude and ignorant times; but it should not encourage similar acts, or criticize judges who had no alternative than to decide as they did.

Socrates did not worship the *deos majorum et minorum gentium*,* but he still attended public sacrifices. Gassendi† went to mass, and Newton attended sermons. Toleration in society should guarantee everyone the freedom to believe what he wishes; but this tolerance should not extend to condoning the effrontery and licence of young hooligans, who wantonly insult what the people revere. These are my sentiments, which accord with the guarantee of public freedom and security, the first object of any legislation.

* The major and minor gods in the hierarchy of classical deities
† Seventeenth-century French scientist and free-thinker

Exercise ══════════════════════════════════════

Compare Frederick's attitude to the Calas affair and the case of De la Barre.

Discussion ══════════════════════════════════════

Frederick shared Voltaire's hatred of religious intolerance and fanaticism; indeed it was Frederick who first described it as '*l'infâme*', a word made famous by Voltaire in his catch-phrase '*Ecrasez l'infâme*' ('Crush the infamous thing'). In a memorial speech to the Berlin Academy on Voltaire's death in 1778, he wrote that, 'had he done no more than to champion the cause of justice and toleration in the Calas, Sirven and De la Barre cases, he would deserve a place among the small number of true benefactors of mankind'. Yet he had no serious wish to extirpate religion, which (notwithstanding document 2) he saw as politically expedient, a social bond and a preserver of law and order; the clergy were useful as teachers and propagandists of obedience and conciliation. Thus while he denounced the Calas affair out of hand—'Calas was innocent; he was the victim of fanaticism'—he saw the case of De la Barre in a different light: De la Barre had provoked his own fate by insulting the established religion—'young hooligans, who wantonly insult what the people revere'.

Frederick's complaint is that De la Barre was guilty of a breach of the peace, outraging law-abiding and respectable citizens. Rejecting crude, overt anticlericalism, Frederick deplored what he regarded as the antireligious 'fanaticism' of the *philosophes*: 'Let us beware of introducing such fanaticism into philosophy, whose character should be mildness and moderation'.

Education

Apart from very brief and insignificant trips to Strasbourg and Holland, Frederick never left Germany. He was thus all the more a remarkable example of a self-taught man, whose broad general knowledge—'encyclopaedic' according to the Prince De Ligne—and lively (if conservative) cultural awareness derived entirely from his own reading. Most of those to whom he demonstrated his learning were foreigners: he held the educational level of his own subjects in low esteem and seems to have regarded himself as the lone 'Philosopher of Sans-Souci' in a kingdom of yahoos. He did little for primary education, which remained under church control and was confined to religious instruction and a 'little reading and writing', 'or else the peasants will all want to leave the countryside to become secretaries'. To Frederick, state education was largely a matter of preparing people for their function in the State according to their class, not of giving them ideas 'above their station'. In 1763 he drew up a detailed scheme of universal education for children from five to thirteen. The nobles were to study separately and middle-class aspirants to the bureaucracy were keen to gain the necessary qualifications. In 1765 Frederick founded the *Académie des Nobles* in Berlin for the specialized training of some twenty young nobles as future officers, diplomats and administrators. The peasants were less well catered for. The provisions for universal education, though impressive on paper, were far inferior to those introduced in Austria, and because Frederick begrudged the funds, there was a chronic lack of trained teachers.

1 Frederick II on enlightenment for the masses

Letter from Frederick II to d'Alembert; 8 January 1770

(*Oeuvres de Frédéric le Grand* Vol XXIV (1854), Berlin, pp. 471–2)

Take any monarchy: let us suppose that it has a population of ten million; of these ten million, let us first discount the farm-labourers, factory-workers, craftsmen and soldiers; that leaves about fifty thousand men and women; from these let us discount twenty-five thousand of the female sex. The rest will consist of the nobility and the upper middle class; of these, let us consider how many ignoramuses there will be, how many idiots, how many imbeciles and loose-livers; and the result of these calculations will be that, in a so-called civilized nation with a population of ten million, you will hardly find a thousand literate people, and even among these, what a difference in talents! Then suppose it were possible that these thousand philosophers all shared the same outlook, and were all equally free from prejudice, what effect would their teaching have on the people? If eight-tenths of the nation, busy gaining a livelihood, do not read at all; if another tenth is too frivolous, debauched or stupid to apply itself, the upshot is that the little good sense of which our species is capable can only reside in a tiny minority of the nation, beyond the reach of the remainder, and that consequently superstitious beliefs will always prevail among the majority . . . Imperfection, moral as well as physical, is the characteristic of the world we live in. It is a waste of energy to try and enlighten it, and sometimes the task is dangerous for those who undertake it. One should content oneself with being wise oneself, if one can be, and abandon the masses to error, while discouraging them from crimes which disturb the social order. Fontenelle* very wisely said that if he had his hand full of truths, he would not open it to impart them to the public, because it was not worth it. I am of roughly the same opinion.

* Popularizer of scientific knowledge and Secretary of the French Academy of Sciences. Author of *Conversations on the Plurality of Worlds* (1686).

Figure 16   Anton Graff, *Frederick the Great*, 1782, oil on canvas—'A decrepit old chatterbox, who ought to be put down' (Frederick the Great). Schloss Charlottenburg Berlin, Elsa Postel.

2   *Frederick II on education for the nobility*

Memorandum; 1765

('Instruction pour la direction de l'Académie des nobles à Berlin', *Oeuvres de Frédéric le Grand* Vol IX (1848), Berlin, pp. 77, 83)

The intention of the King and the purpose of this institution is to educate young gentlemen with a view to qualifying them, according to their vocation, for war or the administration. The masters should therefore strive not merely to fill their minds with useful information but, more particularly, to make them intellectually capable of tackling any subject, and above all to cultivate their reason and form their judgment. They must consequently accustom their pupils to form clear and precise ideas and not to be satisfied with vague and confused ideas . . .

It is forbidden, on pain of imprisonment, for the masters to beat their pupils, who are persons of quality and should be inspired with nobility of soul; they should be punished in ways that arouse ambition, not that humiliate them.

3   *Frederick II on education for the nobility*

Published essay; 18 December 1769

('Lettre sur l'éducation', *Oeuvres de Frédéric le Grand* Vol IX (1848), Berlin, p. 115)

I like to contemplate these young people who are being brought up before our eyes: they are the future generation being inspected by the present generation; a new type of human-being in the making to replace the existing type; the growing hope and strength of the State, who, well led, will perpetuate its splendour and glory. I certainly believe that a wise ruler should make every effort to form in his State useful and virtuous citizens.

Exercise

How would you assess Frederick's views on education?

Discussion

Patronizing and 'elitist' probably describe the sentiments you impute to him. He certainly drew a sharp distinction between the upper classes and the rest, regarding higher education as the preserve of what Gibbon called 'the select few'; the masses should be taught just enough to enable them to perform their duties. Note Frederick's highly sceptical view of mass enlightenment as 'a waste of time'. This view was not as untypical of the period as might be supposed. It was shared explicitly, for example, by Voltaire (see section 5 document 3) and implicitly, it seems to me, by Gibbon (see Units 10–12 pp. 49–50). It is worth noting that in England (though not in Scotland) mass education was not contemplated at all before the second half of the nineteenth century. Frederick perhaps goes somewhat further than Voltaire in his scathing comments on the nobility and his apparent total dismissal of women (though this is surely belied by his lengthy correspondence with the Electress of Saxony, which he clearly enjoyed). For more on Frederick's views of 'enlightenment', see document 4 and section 9. Frederick's provisions for the Noble Academy suggest that he felt a need to encourage some degree of individual judgment and initiative. Note, too, his rejection of corporal punishment as degrading—an exemption which he did not, of course, extend beyond the nobility. There was, then, another side to Frederick's general insistence on unthinking obedience; and he looked ahead to the next generation as 'a new type of human being'. Even here, however, there is no suggestion of any change from absolute rule to some more representative form of government. Guibert provides a significant first-hand description of the Military Academy:

The Military Academy . . . is agreeably situated on the banks of the Spree, opposite to the royal palace. In this school, which is under the wisest and best regulations, fifteen young gentlemen, selected from the corps of noble cadets, are maintained and educated at the King's expense. Their dress, which is a plain uniform, consists of a blue coat, yellow waistcoat and breeches, with white buttons. To every three students an old, sensible and experienced officer is appointed as governor, to be constantly near his pupils and preside over their education. The three pupils sleep together in the same chamber, and have a lacquey in the livery of the house, for their attendant. *The manner in which these young gentlemen are educated is admirably calculated to render them useful members of society and to inspire them with notions suited to their birth; for they are usually of the best families.* They are instructed in all the living languages and in the different sciences, by excellent masters or professors, who are generally members of the Academy of Sciences. Each student has a monthly allowance of nine crowns for pocket money. Their governors are to take care that this money is not expended improperly. In winter they go in a body twice a week to the French comedy; in fine weather they make excursions to the country; one or two of their governors are always of these parties. These gentlemen likewise take it in turns to attend the students to the riding-house and in their other exercises.

Observations on the Military Establishment and Discipline of his Majesty the King of Prussia, translated from the French by J. Johnson, London, 1780, pp. 43–4 (my italics)

The Academy of Sciences

Frederick did little to assist the older, traditional Prussian universities, such as Königsberg and Halle. Instead in 1744 he revived the Berlin *Academy of Sciences and Letters* (originally founded in 1701 by Frederick I with the help of Leibniz) under the presidency of the French scièntist Maupertuis. The aim of the Academy was 'the cultivation of every interesting and useful aspect of the various branches of philosophy, mathematics, physics, natural history, political and literary history, as well as literary criticism'. Its proceedings were usually conducted in French, and its members, appointed by Frederick, were mainly French or French-Swiss. By 1758 only five out of the eighteen academicians were German: Frederick expressly withheld patronage from such notable intellectuals as the playwright, Lessing, the philosopher, Herder, and Winckelmann, the writer on classical art (see Unit 7 Appendix 7, p. 65). This preference for French culture and his recognition that French was the vehicle for Enlightenment thought also reflect Frederick's prejudice against the German language. After Maupertuis' death in 1759, Frederick took personal charge of the Academy, taking occasional advice from d'Alembert (who was secretary of the Académie Française). He never attended the Academy's sessions in person, however, apparently considering that this would detract from his royal dignity: his *Discourse on the Utility of the Arts and Sciences*, delivered on his behalf before the Academy in 1772, demonstrates his wide humanistic interests.

4 Frederick II on progress

Speech to the Academy of Sciences; 27 January 1772

('Discours de l'utilité des sciences et des arts dans un état', *Oeuvres de Frédéric le Grand* Vol IX (1848), Berlin, pp. 171–7)

Some unenlightened or hypocritical persons have ventured to profess their hostility to the arts and sciences. If they have been allowed to slander that which does most honour to humanity, we must be all the more entitled to defend it, for that is the duty of all who love society and who are grateful for what they owe to literature. Unfortunately, paradox often makes a greater impression on the public than truth; it is then that we must disabuse the public and refute the authors of such nonsense, not with insults but with sound reason. I am ashamed to state in this Academy that people have had the effrontery to ask whether the sciences are useful or harmful to society, a subject on which no one should entertain the slightest doubt. If we have any superiority over animals, it is certainly not in our bodily faculties, but in the greater understanding which nature has given us; and what distinguishes one man from another is genius and learning. Where lies the infinite difference between a civilized people and barbarians if not in the fact that the former are enlightened, while the others vegetate in brutish ignorance?

The nations which have enjoyed this superiority have been grateful to those who brought them this advantage. Hence the reputation justly enjoyed by those great thinkers of the world, those sages, who, through their learned works, have enlightened their compatriots and their age.

Man in himself is little enough; he is born with faculties more or less ripe for development. But they require cultivation; his knowledge must increase if his ideas are to broaden; his memory must be filled if it is to supply the imagination with material on which to work, and his judgment must be refined if it is to discriminate between its own products. The greatest mind, without knowledge, is only a rough diamond, which will acquire value only after it has been cut by the hands of a skilled jeweller. What minds have been thus lost to society, what great men of every kind stifled in the bud, whether through ignorance, or through the abject state in which they found themselves placed! Hence the true benefit of the State, its advantage and glory require that the people in it should be as well educated and enlightened as possible, in order to furnish it, in every field, with a number of trained subjects capable of acquitting themselves expertly in the different tasks entrusted to them. . .

OEUVRES
DU PHILOSOPHE
DE
SANS-SOUCI.

SECONDE EDITION.

FRIDERICUS REX

A POTZDAM,

M. DCC. LX.

There are some false political thinkers, limited by their narrow ideas, who, without going deeply into the matter, have supposed that it is easier to rule an ignorant and stupid people than an enlightened nation. That is a really powerful argument, when experience proves that the more brutish the people are, the more they are capricious and obstinate, and that it is far more difficult to overcome its obstinacy than to explain realities to a people civilized enough to listen to reason! It would be a fine country where talents remained forever stifled and where there was only one man less narrow-minded than the rest! Such a state, inhabited by ignoramuses, would be like the lost paradise in Genesis, inhabited only by animals.

Although it is unnecessary to demonstrate to this illustrious audience and in this Academy that the arts and sciences bring both utility and fame to the peoples who possess them, it will perhaps not be without use to convince some less enlightened persons of the same thing, to arm them against the effects which some vile sophists might have on their minds. Let them compare a Canadian savage with any citizen of a civilized country of Europe, and all the advantage will be with the latter. How can one prefer crude nature to nature perfected, lack of means of subsistence to a life of ease, rudeness to politeness, security of possessions enjoyed under the protection of the laws to the law of the jungle and to anarchy, which destroys the fortunes and conditions of families?

Society, a community of men, could not do without either the arts or the sciences. Thanks to surveying and hydraulics, riparian regions are protected from flooding; without these arts, fertile lands would become unhealthy marshes, and would deprive numerous families of their livelihood. The higher lands could not do without surveyors to measure out and divide the fields. The physical sciences, firmly established by experiment, help to perfect agriculture and, in particular, horticulture. Botany, applied to the study of medicinal herbs, and chemistry, which can extract their essences, serve at least to fortify our hope during our illnesses, even if their property cannot cure us. Anatomy guides and directs the surgeon's hand in those painful but necessary operations that save our life at the price of an amputated limb.

The mechanical sciences are useful in every field. If a load is to be raised or transported, they will move it. If we are to dig into the bowels of the earth to extract metals, the science of mechanics, with ingenious machines, pumps out the quarries and frees the miner from the superabundance of water which would cost him his life or his work. If we need mills to grind the most familiar and basic form of food, the science of mechanics perfects them. It is the science of mechanics that helps craftsmen by improving the various kinds of craft at which they work. Every kind of machine lies within its province. And how many machines are needed in all the various fields! The craft of shipbuilding constitutes perhaps one of the greatest efforts of imagination; but how much knowledge the pilot must possess to steer his ship and brave wind and wave! He needs to have studied astronomy, to have good charts, an exact knowledge of geography and arithmetical skill, in order to ascertain the distance he has travelled and the point at which he is, and in this respect he will be helped in future by the chronometers that have just been perfected in England. The arts and sciences go hand in hand: we owe them everything, they are the benefactors of mankind . . .

We agree that logic is beyond the riff-raff; this large section of the human race will always be the last to open its eyes to facts; but although in every country, it retains a store of superstitions, it is also true to say that we have succeeded in disabusing it of its belief in witches, possession by devils, the philosopher's stone and other equally childish nonsense. We owe these advantages to the more meticulous study of nature which has been carried out. Physics has been combined with analysis and experiment; the brightest light has been brought to bear among those dark places which concealed so many truths from scholars of the past; and although we cannot attain to the knowledge of the first secret principles, which the Great Geometer has reserved for himself alone, powerful geniuses have arisen who discovered the laws of gravity and motion. Chancellor Bacon, the precursor of the new philosophy, or rather, the man who guessed and predicted its progress, put Sir Isaac Newton on the track of his marvellous discoveries; Newton appeared after Descartes, who, having discredited the errors of the past, replaced them with errors of his own.[11] Since then, men have weighed the air, measured the skies, calculated the movement of the heavenly bodies with infinite accuracy, predicted eclipses, and discovered an unknown property of matter, the force of electricity, whose effects astound the imagination; and doubtless men will soon be able to predict the appearance of comets, as they do that of eclipses (though we already owe to the learned Bayle★ the dissipation of the fear which this phenomenon caused among the ignorant). Let us admit: while the weakness of our condition makes us humble, the works of these great men restore our courage and make us feel the dignity of our being.

★ In his *Miscellaneous Thoughts on the Comet of 1680*: '. . . wherein it is proved by several reasons drawn from philosophy and theology that comets are not presages of misfortunes'.

Exercise

What is Frederick's main point in his *Discourse on the Utility of the Arts and Sciences*?

Specimen answer and discussion

Frederick is defending the concept of civilization and the doctrine of the possibility of human progress through scientific, technological and material advance. This idea was the main inspiration behind the *Encyclopédie* (see, for example, d'Alembert's *Preliminary Discourse* (Course Anthology Vol 2 pp. 126–43 and Units 13–14) and compare Gibbon (chapter XXXVIII Course Anthology Vol 1, pp. 325–32 and Units 10–12 pp. 74–6)).

Frederick is also making a direct attack on the ideas of Rousseau. In 1750 the Academy of Dijon set an essay competition on the subject: 'Whether the restoration of the arts and sciences has helped to improve morals'. In his prize-winning essay,

[11] For Bacon, Newton and Descartes, see Units 13–14, The 'Encyclopédie'.

published as the *Discourse on the Arts and Sciences*, and his later *Discourse on Inequality* (1753), Rousseau produced a dramatic and radical critique of the idea of material progress. Far from being conducive to human happiness, he argued, material advance leads to luxury, decadence, social injustice and national decline. Rousseau called for a return to something approaching Spartan austerity and virtue.

For what was seen as his perverse obscurantism and his betrayal of their cause, Rousseau was ostracized, criticized and ridiculed by the *philosophes*, notably Voltaire, and is here accused by Frederick of publicity-mongering: 'unfortunately paradox often makes a greater impression on the public than truth' (see radio programme 18, 'Rousseau and the Enlightenment' and television programme 7, 'Dinner at Baron D'Holbach's'). Note that Frederick here qualifies his earlier sceptical comments on general enlightenment expressed in document 1. He agrees that the people 'should be as well educated and enlightened as possible.' However, 'as possible' doubtless contains a significant implied reservation.

Medical progress

Smallpox was a major scourge in the eighteenth century until relieved by the use of inoculation, (propagandized by Voltaire and in the *Encyclopédie*). Even so, sharp hostility to inoculation prevailed among the authorities in Catholic states, such as France, Austria and Spain, in each of which members of the royal family, having refused inoculation as contrary to God's will, fell victim to smallpox. The most eminent of these victims was Louis XV, who died in 1774. Frederick's scientific, rational outlook and policy contrast with this obscurantism.

5 *Frederick II on inoculation*

Letter from Frederick II to Electress Maria Antonia of Saxony; 26 July 1763

(*Oeuvres de Frédéric le Grand* Vol XXIV (1854), Berlin, pp. 41–2)

I learn with pleasure, Madam, that your family has been successfully inoculated against smallpox, and I offer you my sincere congratulations. The Paris *Parlement* has just pronounced judgment against this practice, so hard it is to destroy old, ignorant prejudices, and so much time is needed before men will do anything rational. However, the Duke of Orleans has had his children successfully inoculated; of a million people who have been inoculated at Berlin, no one has died; and after so many examples, it really is time to renounce such absurd rulings, which reflect so badly on the judges.

6 *Maria Antonia on inoculation*

Letter from Electress Maria Antonia of Saxony to Frederick II; 5 August 1763

(*Oeuvres de Frédéric le Grand* Vol XXIV (1854), Berlin, p. 42–3)

As for inoculation, it is to you, Sire, that I owe the courage I had in arranging for my family to undergo it. It was you who encouraged me and persuaded the Prince-Elector to allow it. So I owe to you the preservation of my children's lives, and Saxony will owe to you the lives of thousands of children whose parents are following my example. Like your Majesty, I am astonished that doctors as enlightened as those of the Sorbonne have been so enslaved by ancient maxims as to forbid a practice so salutory. My own doctors, and the local priests in particular, did not wish to allow it either; but since my example has been a sort of authorization, people are doing without their permission, and almost all the nobility of Saxony has followed my example.

Freedom of expression

7 *Frederick II on freedom of expression*

B. H. Latrobe (ed) *Characteristic Anecdotes and Miscellaneous Authentic Papers of Frederick II* (1788), London, pp. 137–9

The King once observed from a window in the palace that a great concourse of people were reading something stuck up against a wall; and he sent one of his pages down to see what it was. The page returned and informed him that the paper contained satirical observations upon the new regulations in the collection of the duties upon coffee.* 'Go down again', said the King, 'and get the bill pasted lower, that they may read it more conveniently; it is too high for them.'

* A cartoon showing Frederick grinding a coffee-mill and picking up spilled beans

Frederick showed amazing indifference to verbal attacks on his own person. This is attested by Dr Moore:

> Nothing surprised me more, when I first came to Berlin, than the freedom with which many people speak of the measures of government and the conduct of the King. I have heard political topics and others which I should have thought still more ticklish, discussed here with as little ceremony as at a London coffee-house. The same freedom appears in the booksellers' shops, where literary productions of all kinds are sold openly. The pamphlet lately published on the division of Poland, wherein the King is very roughly treated, is to be had without difficulty, as well as other performances, which attack some of the most conspicuous characters with all the bitterness of satire.
>
> *A View of Society and Manners in France, Switzerland and Germany*, Vol II (1789), Dublin, p. 130

Perhaps Frederick made a virtue of necessity: it would have been impractical and undignified to attempt to stem the influx of broadsheets from outside Prussia. He did not allow complete freedom of expression, however. While universities and the Academy were free from censorship, the law prescribed strict penalties against the criticism of political conditions or complaints against army life. Probably Frederick was concerned to preserve public order and prevent alarm and despondency, rather than to suppress ideas as such. But intellectuals like Lessing and Winckelmann complained of a lack of genuine freedom in Prussia. Lessing wrote in 1769: 'Do not talk to me of your freedom of thought. It boils down to permission to let off as many squibs as you like against religion. Let someone raise his voice for the rights of subjects or against exploitation and despotism, and you will soon see which is the most slavish country in Europe.'

Literature and Augustanism

Frederick was a devotee of French literature and a prolific writer of French verse and prose, who aspired to win literary fame in his own right; he shared the veneration of the age for Voltaire the writer, despite his reservations about Voltaire the man and their checkered personal encounter (see television programme 8, 'Frederick and Voltaire'). Their correspondence lasted for half a century and fills three volumes. Frederick regarded Voltaire not only as a brilliant purveyor of Enlightenment ideas, but still more as the only contemporary writer who successfully emulated the 'Augustan' styles and standards of literary excellence achieved by the writers of the age of Louis XIV. In 1770 d'Alembert invited Frederick to contribute to the commissioning of a statue of Voltaire by the sculptor Pigalle. Frederick's gracious reply was read before the Académie Française and formally recorded in its *Proceedings*.

8 *Frederick II on French literature*

Letter from Frederick II to Voltaire; *c* 20 August 1766

(T. Besterman (ed) *Voltaire's Correspondence* Vol LXII (1961), Geneva, p. 132)

If you have any new work available, kindly send it on to me. The books that come out these days make one long for those of the beginning of the century. . . You no longer have any dramatic poets in France, or those pretty society verses that one used to see such a lot of formerly. I note an analytical and geometrical spirit in everything that is written; but literature is in its decline. There are no more celebrated orators, no more light verse, none of those charming works which used once to be part of the glory of the French nation. You, Monsieur, are the last to have maintained that glory; but you will have no successors. Live, therefore, a long and healthy life.

9 D'Alembert on Voltaire

Letter from d'Alembert to Frederick II; 6 July 1770

(*Oeuvres de Frédéric le Grand* Vol XXIV (1854), Berlin, pp. 488–9)

An important society of philosophers and men of letters, including myself, has decided, Sire, to erect a statue in honour of Monsieur de Voltaire, the man to whom our writers of philosophy and literature are most particularly indebted.

The *philosophes* and men of letters of every nation, and of France in particular, have long regarded you, Sire, as their leader and their model. How flattering and what an honour then it would be for us, if on this occasion Your Majesty would allow your august and respectable name to appear at the head of our list. You would give to Monsieur de Voltaire, whose works you favour so much, the most precious and brilliant token of esteem, which would infinitely move him and would make the remainder of his days dear to him. You would add greatly to the glory of this celebrated writer and to that of French literature, which would remain eternally grateful.

Figure 18 Bronze bust of Voltaire by Jean-Antoine Houdon (1741–1828), now in the Louvre. 'A pity such a wonderful genius should be combined with such a bad character' (Frederick the Great). Radio Times Hulton Picture Library.

10 Frederick II on Voltaire

Letter from Frederick II to d'Alembert; 28 July 1770

(*Oeuvres de Frédéric le Grand* Vol XXIV (1854), Berlin, pp. 491–2)

Voltaire's finest monument is that which he has created himself—his works, which will outlast the Basilica of St Peter's, the Louvre, and all those buildings that human vanity supposes will last forever. When French is no longer spoken, Voltaire will still be translated into the language that succeeds to French. Moreover, filled as I am with the pleasure that his works have given me, so varied and so perfect, each in its kind, I could not without ingratitude decline your proposal that I contribute to the monument which a grateful public is erecting in his honour. You have only to tell me what is required of me. I shall refuse nothing for that statue, which will do more honour to the men of letters who are consecrating it to him, than to Voltaire himself. Men will say that in this eighteenth century, when so many men of letters were riven with envy, there were some noble enough and generous enough to do justice to a man endowed with greater genius and talents than in any century; that we deserved to have Voltaire; and even the remotest posterity will envy us that advantage. To distinguish celebrated men, to do justice to merit, is to encourage talent and virtue and is the sole reward of great minds; it is certainly owed to all those who cultivate literature superlatively well. Literature brings us pleasures of the mind, more lasting than those of the body; it softens the harshest manners, it spreads its charms across the whole course of life; it makes life tolerable, and death less frightful. Continue, then, gentlemen, to protect and celebrate its practitioners, so eminently successful as they are in France: it will be the most glorious thing you can do for your nation and will win the gratitude of future ages.

Some scholars dismiss Frederick's francophile tastes as little more than a façade, perhaps even an affectation, without underlying significance. 'The Gallic and rococo veneer', says the American scholar Gershoy, 'was a thin gloss over a great body of barrack brutality.' It is true that French language and culture prevailed in the German courts as in the European capitals generally, with the absence of a native German literature before *c* 1750, so that Frederick was by no means unique in his tastes. But 'a thin gloss'? Surely his feeling for French language and culture went deeper than that?

French culture for Frederick was also a means of escape from and opposition to his father's hostility to 'French ways', a way of expressing his own individuality and his love of artistic and civilized values. French thought also enabled Frederick to view conditions in Prussia from a new, more objective perspective. As Ritter argues:

> Had Frederick followed the wishes of his father and grown up to be a well-meaning, pious and paternal German ruler, conditions in Prussia presumably would have remained unchanged. No doubt life would have been peaceful; but the state would never have risen to great political power. Only by tearing himself away from his native tradition was Frederick able to gain the inner freedom to set out on the dangerous and glorious road that carried him far beyond his predecessors. And he achieved this liberation only with the help of the ideas of the European Enlightenment.
>
> *Frederick the Great: an Historical Profile* p. 48

Note Frederick's observations on the immortality of literature. The desire for posthumous literary glory was common in the eighteenth century (compare, for example, Fielding's *Tom Jones*, Book VIII chapter 1); and Frederick's idea that literary glory is more durable than architectural glory (which derives from Horace's *Odes*, III, xxx) is parallelled in Gibbon's famous praise of Fielding: 'The romance of *Tom Jones* . . . will outlive the palace of the Escorial and the Imperial Eagle of the House of Austria'. Frederick once claimed that he would rather have been the author of a single line of Racine than have won his most outstanding victories. His respect for literary greatness, and the humanizing influence that he ascribes to literature, were surely characteristic of his total outlook and went deeper than mere affectation or literary convention?

Classical civilization

The following document (which you may remember from Units 10–12 p. 14) shows Frederick apparently as familiar with the history and topography of Rome as if he had visited it and as much a Latinist as Gibbon, whose *Decline and Fall of the Roman Empire* he regretted not having time to read (even in a French translation). In fact Frederick never visited Italy and his occasional Latin tags were full of schoolboy howlers; his father, it will be remembered, had actually forbidden him to learn Latin as a boy. However, he had an excellent knowledge of the classics through French translations.

As we have seen earlier (section 1 document 5), the Romans are held out by Frederick as models of *humanitas*, combining literary cultivation with the stoic characteristics of 'virtue', 'courage', 'wisdom' and 'statesmanship'.

11   Frederick II on ancient Rome

Letter from Frederick II to Electress Maria Antonia of Saxony; 22 March 1772

(*Oeuvres de Frédéric le Grand* Vol XXIV (1854), Berlin, p. 238)

It is a sight worthy of the enlightened eyes of Your Royal Highness to behold even the remains of the former greatness of the Romans. You will see the Capitol, where the conquerors of the world held their triumphs; you will see the sites of the ancient rostra, where Cicero declaimed . . . ; you will see the ruins of the vast amphitheatres, where as many as sixty thousand spectators assembled; the theatres, where Roscius and Aesop performed in front of Cato, Pompey and Caesar; the places where Virgil recited his *Aeneid* or Horace sang his *Odes*; in a word, the seat of the mightiest empire known to the world; renowned for the virtue and courage of so many Roman ladies who contributed, like the patricians, to the good of the State; in a word, where everything combined to raise that nation above all those of the known world. And what spectacle more interesting than to reflect that even after the fall of that vast empire, the wisdom of the Romans could actually regain through statesmanship and the minds of men (which it was able to influence) what it had lost by the sword of the barbarians who subjugated them.

German literature

Frederick had little time for German literature, which was just beginning to emerge around the mid-century. 'Since my youth I have not read a German book', he said in 1757; 'now that I am an old fellow, I have no time.' While subsidizing the often second-rate foreign members of his Academy, he scorned native writers like Lessing, whose ideas on military honour (as in the first original German comedy, *Minha von Barnhelm*, 1767) and religious toleration (as in *Nathan the Wise*, 1779) might have been expected to appeal to him. As for the new pre-romantic movement of younger writers, known as '*Sturm und Drang*' ('Storm and stress'), Frederick had nothing but contempt. He poured scorn on Goethe's immensely popular novel of sentimental love, *The Sorrows of Young Werther* (1774), and his full-blooded historical melodrama, *Götz von Berlichingen* (1773) he lambasted as an 'abominable imitation' of 'Shakespeare's bizarre aberrations'. Of Shakespeare's own works, which were beginning to appear in translation, Frederick said that they were 'ridiculous farces, worthy of Canadian savages'. As an inveterate devotee of classicism, what appalled him about Shakespeare and the *Sturm und Drang* writers was their disregard of the canons of Augustan taste, epitomized for him in his favourite poet, the French tragedian Racine, and the other classic authors of the age of Louis XIV. When taxed by Mirabeau with his failure to encourage German literature, Frederick replied, perhaps somewhat disingenuously, that his greatest service to German writers had been to leave them alone. Despite his Augustan predilections, and his ignorance of the native German Enlightenment coming to bloom during his reign (the *Aufklärung*, see Course Guide and Course Anthology Vol 2, pp. 249–55), he did hold out hopes of an eventual flowering of letters in Germany.

12   Frederick II on German literature

Letter from Frederick II to Voltaire; 24 July 1775

(T. Besterman (ed) *Voltaire's Correspondence* Vol XCI (1964), Geneva, p. 121)

The Germans are aspiring to enjoy in their turn the benefits of the fine arts. They strive to equal Athens, Rome, Florence and Paris. For all my love of my native land, I cannot say that they have so far succeeded. They lack two things: language and taste. The language is too wordy; good society speaks French; and a few pedantic schoolmasters and professors cannot give German the politeness and easy turns-of-phrase that it can only acquire in high society. In addition, there is the variety of idioms: each province has its own, and so far no rules of preference have been laid down. As for taste, the Germans are particularly lacking in that. They have still not been able to imitate the authors of the age of Augustus; they produce a vicious mixture of Roman taste with English, French and Teutonic. They still lack that fine discernment which seizes on beauty where it finds it and can distinguish the commonplace from the perfect, the noble from the sublime, and can apply each of them in the right places. As long as there are plenty of 'r's in their poetic vocabulary, they consider their verses harmonious; while as a rule they are only a meaningless jumble of puffed-up verbiage. As far as history is concerned, they will not omit the slightest detail, however insignificant.

Their best works are on Public Law. As for philosophy, since the genius of Leibniz[12] and the great monad of Wolff,* nobody tackles it any more. They imagine they are successful in drama, but so far nothing perfect has appeared. Germany at the present day is at exactly the same stage as France in the time of François I.† The taste for literature is starting to spread; we must wait for nature to bring forth some real geniuses, as happened under Richelieu** and Mazarin.†† The soil that produced a Leibniz can produce others.

I shall not live to see these fine days for my native land, but I foresee their possibility.

*   Popularizer of the philosophy of Leibniz (see Units 19–20 p. 10) in which the basic element of being was called the 'monad'.
†   Ruled 1515–1547.
** Minister 1624–42 and founder of the Académie Française.
†† Minister 1643–61

13   Frederick II on German literature

Letter from Frederick II to Voltaire; 8 September 1775

(T. Besterman (ed) *Voltaire's Correspondence* Vol XCII (1964), Geneva, pp. 14–15)

Taste will only spread in Germany after careful study of the classic writers, Greek as well as Roman and French. Two or three men of genius will improve the language and make it less barbarous, and will naturalize the foreign masterpieces in Germany. As for me, whose career is approaching its end, I shall not live to see those happy times. I would like to have contributed to their birth; but what could I do, a being preoccupied for two thirds of his career by continual wars, obliged to repair the evils caused by them, and born with talents too slight for such tasks? Philosophy comes to us from Epicurus; Gassendi, Newton and Locke improved it; I do myself the honour of being their disciple, but no more.

Exercise══

Explain Frederick's reference to the 'authors of the age of Augustus' (document 12).

Specimen answer══════════════════════════════════

This should have presented little difficulty to you after the Pope and Gibbon units. Frederick means such writers as Livy, Virgil and Horace. (His own favourite classical authors include Cicero, Plutarch, Lucretius, Suetonius and Tacitus.) In general Frederick implies the absolute superiority of the 'Augustan' standards of the

[12] See Units 13–14 pp. 72–74.

age of Louis XIV so much admired in the eighteenth century as models of elegance, proportion and harmony.

Note that 'good society speaks French', and Frederick's characteristic insistence that 'taste will only spread in Germany after careful study of the classic writers, Greek as well as Roman and French'. 'Athens, Rome, Florence and Paris' represented the peaks of civilization and cultural achievement in the eyes of Enlightenment historians (see Units 10–12 pp. 62–4). Frederick's aristocratic adherence to classicism and the noble style in literature perhaps also mirrors his social conservatism: the contemporary *Sturm and Drang* writers were beginning to concern themselves with the lives of non-nobles, and even with 'low life'.

Music

Frederick's musical tastes were also rooted in the past. He only liked instrumental music that included a flute part, which he would perform himself with great virtuosity according to the English musicologist, Dr Burney, who heard him in 1772. These performances included original compositions by Frederick and some 300 flute concertos by his court composer and tutor, J. J. Quantz. Frederick's other passion was for early eighteenth-century Italianate grand opera in the style popularized by Handel: in particular the operas of the Neapolitan composer, Vinci, and the Germans, Graun, (another court musician at Sans-Souci), and Hasse, a pupil of Alessandro Scarlatti. Hasse's operas, notably *Cleophides*, first produced in 1731, were revived throughout the reign at the Berlin Opera House, founded by Frederick in 1742. Another court musician at Sans-Souci was C. P. E. Bach, son of the great J. S. Bach, and an important, even revolutionary, composer in his own right. Frederick ignored his aspirations as a composer, however, dismissing all modern music as decadent, and retained C. P. E. Bach simply as harpsichord-accompanist to his own flute performances.

14 *Frederick II on music*

Letter from Frederick II to Electress Maria Antonia of Saxony; 8 January 1777

(*Oeuvres de Frédéric le Grand* Vol XXIV (1854), Berlin, p. 292)

The public here is enjoying the opera *Cleophides*, by Hasse, which has been revived again. Good things are always good; even though one has heard them before, one still enjoys hearing them again. Besides, modern music has degenerated into mere cacophany, earsplitting rather than harmonious; and grand opera is now beyond our contemporaries. In order to recapture it, one must return to Vinci, Hasse and Graun.

Dr Burney commented in 1772 on Frederick's conservative—and dictatorial—tastes in music:

> Upon the whole, my expectations from Berlin were not quite answered, as I did not find that the style of composition or manner of execution to which his Prussian Majesty has attached himself, fulfilled my ideas of perfection . . . I speak according to my own feelings; however it would be a presumption in me to oppose my single judgment to that of so enlightened a prince, if, luckily, mine were not the opinion of the greatest part of Europe. For, should it be allowed that his Prussian Majesty has fixed upon the Augustan age of music, it does not appear that he has placed his favour upon the best composers of that age. Vinci, Pergolesi . . . Handel and many others, who flourished in the best times of Graun and Quantz, I think superior to them in taste and genius. Of his Majesty's two favourites, the one is languid, and the other frequently common and insipid—and yet their names are religion at Berlin . . . Though a universal toleration prevails here as to different sects of Christians, yet in music, whoever dares to profess any other tenets than those of Graun and Quantz, is sure to be persecuted.

Figure 19 Aria from Hasse's opera *Cleophides* (1731) scored by Frederick the Great in his own hand. 'Negotiations without arms are as effective as music scores without instruments' (Frederick the Great). Wiesbaden, Akademische Verlagsgesellschaft Athenaion.

Though there are constantly Italian operas here in carnival time, his Prussian Majesty will suffer none to be performed but those of Graun, . . . or Hasse, and of this last, and best, but very few. And in the opera house, as in the field, his Majesty is such a rigid disciplinarian, that if a mistake is made in a single movement or evolution, he immediately marks, and rebukes the offender; and if any of his Italian troops dare to deviate from strict discipline, by adding, altering or diminishing a single passage in the parts they have to perform, an order is sent, *de par le Roi* [by order of the King], for them to adhere strictly to the notes written by the composer, at their peril . . . So that music is truly stationary in this country, his Majesty allowing no more liberty in that than he does in civil matters of government. Not contented with being sole master of the lives, fortunes and business of his subjects, he even prescribes rules to their most innocent pleasures.

'The Present State of Music in Germany', in P. Scholes (ed) *Dr Burney's Musical Tours in Europe* Vol II (1959), Oxford University Press, p. 207

Architecture

15 *Frederick II on Architecture*

Diary entry of De Catt; 27 April 1758

(By H. De Catt, in R. Koser (ed) *Unterhaltungen mit Friedrich dem Grossen. Memoiren und Tagebücher von Heinrich de Catt, Publicationen aus den Königlichen Preussischen Staatsarchiven* Vol XXII (1884), Leipzig, p. 38)

Potsdam, Potsdam—there is where we must be to be happy. When you* see this town, I am sure you will like it. It was a shanty-town in my father's time; if he went back there, he would certainly not recognize the place any more, I have embellished it so much. I have chosen the plans from among the finest architectural designs in Europe, and Italy in particular; I have had them carried out on a small scale according to my means. The proportions are well observed, and all the buildings that I have had put up are interesting, you will agree. I love building and decorating, I admit, but I do it from my savings, and the State does not suffer as a result; by my building schemes, I provide employment, which is most important in a State; nothing is more fatal than to tolerate idleness and support useless people. The State suffers from it more than I could tell you. The money I spend on my buildings stays in the country and circulates; and this is yet another advantage that I gain from my way of building. You have no idea how much money I have spent to make my Potsdam agreeable, I would be ashamed to tell you how much my Sans-Souci costs me; I would always regret what I have spent on it in pictures, statues, antiques, colonnades and gardens, if, as I said, I had not done it all out of my own small savings.

* Henri De Catt, a Swiss, Frederick's literary secretary, employed to read to Frederick in French.

7 War and Peace: Foreign Policy

War and peace

There was a constant oscillation in Frederick's thinking between the ideal claims of humanitarianism and the actual requirements of the State. Professor Holborn comments:

> It was paradoxical that the Age of Enlightenment, with its strong cosmopolitan feeling among the educated people, should have banned any deeper European loyalties from politics. But the very rationalism that helped create the new cosmopolitan faith in humanity turned the states into separate machines of power to be run according to technical rules. Mercantilism strengthened this political insulation and cut the ties between the nations.
>
> *A History of Modern Germany 1648–1840*(1965). Eyre and Spottiswoode, London, p. 241

While holding genuinely to ideals of human dignity, culture and civilization, Frederick was convinced that the only unit that could provide the conditions in which such ideals might be realized was the State. But given the existing conditions of international relations, the State, he believed, had to be strong, secure and united, able to deter or to withstand aggression. Prussia was geographically truncated (a 'kingdom of border-strips' in Voltaire's phrase, 'spider's legs without a body' in that of a modern historian) and surrounded by powerful neighbours; it was therefore chronically vulnerable to invasion and liable in the event of defeat to that ultimate fate of losing states in the eighteenth century—partition. Indeed, in the Seven Years War (1756–63) East Prussia was annexed by Russia. Simply to survive, as Frederick saw it, Prussia must at all costs round off her vulnerable frontiers and consolidate her scattered territories by expansion. Inevitably this had to be at the expense of other states and therefore involve a power struggle. If possible, expansion should be achieved by diplomatic means, but successful diplomacy, in Frederick's view, needed to be backed by the threat of overwhelming military strength (as in the partition of Poland in 1772). Alternatively, expansion could be brought about by direct military conflict, provided that this was likely to succeed without excessive cost (as in the invasion of Silesia in 1740). Hence Frederick's ultimate conviction was of the need to postpone policies based on Enlightenment ideals until such time as Prussia was strong enough to guarantee their realization; he constantly subordinated humanitarian ethics to his perception of the immediate needs of the State.

Under Frederick-William I, despite a colossal build-up of troops, Prussia had played a passive and even ignominious role in German affairs as little more than a tool of Austria. Frederick reversed this: beginning with his invasion of Silesia in 1740, Prussia was henceforth to take the initiative in Germany.

As in all other aspects of government, Frederick was sole master of his foreign policy. He often bypassed his own Foreign Office, corresponding directly with his ambassadors and agents abroad. His foreign minister, Podewils, who ventured to oppose the invasion of Saxony in 1756 (the move that precipitated the Seven Years War), was instantly dismissed—'A wet hen', Frederick called him.

Frederick's *Anti-Machiavel* (or *Refutation of Machiavelli*) (corrected and polished by Voltaire, who also arranged its publication in Holland in 1740) is largely a conventional humanitarian critique of war, an 'edifying homily' (Macaulay), though it did provide for the waging of a 'just war' where the safety of the State demanded it. This expression of pacifist sentiment was followed so swiftly by Frederick's invasion of Silesia, that both Voltaire and Rousseau observed that to publish a book against Machiavelli, and thus throw one's enemies off-guard, was itself a Machiavellian ploy.

1   Frederick II on war

Published treatise; 1740

('La réfutation du Prince De Machiavel', in C. Fleischauer (ed) *Studies on Voltaire and the Eighteenth Century* Vol 5 (1958), Geneva, pp. 180, 352–5)

I ask: what can be the motive that makes a man seek to aggrandize himself? What can be his reason for plotting to base his power on the misery and destruction of others, and how can he believe that he will make a name for himself by merely making men unhappy? A monarch's fresh conquests do not make his existing possessions any richer; his peoples gain nothing from them, and he deceives himself if he imagines that they will make him any happier. . .

War is so rich in misfortunes, its outcome is so uncertain and its consequences are so disastrous for a country, that rulers can hardly reflect too long before embarking on it. I say nothing of the injustice and violence that they do to their neighbours, but confine myself to the miseries that fall directly upon their own subjects. I am convinced that if kings and rulers had a true picture of the people's sufferings, they would not be unmoved by them. But they lack the imagination to form an objective idea of the evils from which their status shields them. A ruler should be made to realize that his burning ambition sparks off all the fatal consequences to which war is prone; the taxes that cripple the people; the levies that deprive the country of all its young men; the epidemics that sweep through armies, where so many die in misery; the murderous sieges; the still crueller battles; the wounded, whom the loss of some limb deprives of the only means of subsistence, and the orphans, from whom the enemy fire has snatched those

Figure 20   Title page of Frederick the Great's *Examen du Prince de Machiavel . . . (The Anti-Machiavel)*, 1741. 'If Machiavelli had had a prince as a pupil, the first thing he would have recommended would be that he write against Machiavelli' (Voltaire). Reproduced by permission of the British Library Board.

who braved the dangers and sold to the ruler their lives and their sustinence. So many men, useful to the State, cut off before their time! Never was there a tyrant who committed such cruelties in cold blood. Rulers who wage unjust wars are crueller than they. They sacrifice to their impetuous passion the happiness, health and the lives of an infinite number of men, whom it was their duty to protect and make happy, instead of so recklessly exposing them to everything that humanity has most to fear. It is therefore certain that the world's rulers cannot be too prudent and cautious in their actions, and cannot be too careful for the lives of their subjects, whom they should not regard as their slaves, but as their equals, and in a certain sense, as their masters.

Exercise

On the basis of document 1, do you think Voltaire and Rousseau were correct in seeing the book as a Machiavellian ruse?

Specimen answer and discussion

You should know enough about Frederick by now not to dismiss a Machiavellian motive out of hand. But equally, the passage expresses an aspect of Frederick that you should also recognize as genuine, indeed as the basis of much of his achievement—his active sense of responsibility for the welfare of his people. It is quite possible that the *Anti-Machiavel* was a sincere tract against war, conquest and vainglory, of a type that was common in contemporary writing (see Voltaire's article on war, document 6) and which Frederick believed when he wrote it.

On closer examination, however, it seems to me that what Frederick is criticizing is not war in general, but rather unnecessary and unjust wars, i.e. wars begun out of personal motives and for insufficient reasons, such as those embarked on in order to satisfy the ambition of the ruler rather than the needs of the State. Frederick says that 'rulers can hardly reflect too long before embarking on it'; he does not say that they should never embark on it at all. He seems to be arguing against the reckless, irrational and uneconomic waging of war, the implication being that war should only be begun after a careful weighing-up of all the pros and cons, and should be waged as economically and humanely as possible.

2   Frederick II on war and peace

Letter from Frederick II to Voltaire; 2 July 1759

(T. Besterman (ed) *Voltaire's Correspondence* Vol XXXVI (1958), Geneva, pp. 203–4)

I love peace just as much as you; but I want it to be good, solid and honourable. Socrates and Plato would have thought as I do, had they found themselves in my wretched plight. Do you suppose there is any pleasure in this dog's life, slaughtering foreigners, losing your friends and acquaintances every day, seeing your reputation continually exposed to the caprices of Fortune, spending the whole year in anxiety and apprehension, endlessly risking life and fortune? Certainly I know the value of peace, the joys of society, the pleasures of life; and I like to be happy as much as anyone. But however much I yearn for all these blessings, I will not purchase them at the price of baseness and infamy. Philosophy teaches us to do our duty, to serve our country faithfully, at the cost of our repose, and if need be, of our life, to sacrifice our whole being for it. The illustrious Zadig★ underwent many adventures that were not to his taste; Candide likewise; but they accepted their lot patiently. What finer example to follow than that of those heroes?

★ Hero of Voltaire's philosophical tale of the same name (1747)

3   Frederick II on war and peace

Letter from Frederick II to Electress Maria Antonia of Saxony; 18 May 1764

(*Oeuvres de Frédéric le Grand* Vol XXIV (1854), Berlin, p. 66)

Your sentiments in favour of peace are certainly the same as those that I have long entertained. I look on war, Madam, as an evil that is sometimes necessary, when negotiations and the paths of conciliation have gone as far as they can. But I am firmly of the opinion that even when one is forced to take this violent step, it should only be with a view to restoring peace as soon as possible.

4 Frederick II on raison d'état

Letter from Frederick II to Electress Maria Antonia of Saxony; 8 March 1766

(*Oeuvres de Frédéric le Grand* Vol XXIV (1854), Berlin, p. 109)

Certainly, Madam, no society can exist without justice. Do unto others what you would have them do to you; this principle embodies the whole of virtue and Man's duties towards the society in which he lives. That is the basis of that Public Law so well known in the German universities, but which is nearly always crushed by the law of the heavy guns. Thus, Madam, men's reason and their passion are constantly opposed to each other, and what the one sets up, the other knocks down. As for those, Madam, who are in charge of government, I think one should hear them before condemning them. I certainly do not regard these people as despots; if they are, it is only when they abuse their position. Their position places them in charge of society and their basic duty is to further to the utmost of their ability the interests of that nation, that is to say, to maintain the security of its possessions, which is the first right of every citizen; next, to protect it from the designs of neighbours who seek to harm it, and lastly to defend it against enemy aggression. Now, Madam, put the mildest and most impartial man in charge of this task, and you will agree that in order to discharge his duties, he must act in a different way from that which his natural inclination would dictate. He is like a tutor, who though generous as far as his own interests are concerned, is jealously concerned for those of his pupil. That, Madam, is my idea of the duty of monarchs, and so that is the basis upon which I act in my own small sphere.

5 Frederick II on raison d'état

Letter from Frederick II to Electress Maria Antonia of Saxony; 16 April 1766

(*Oeuvres de Frédéric le Grand* Vol XXIV (1854), Berlin, pp. 111–2)

Certainly, Madam, our humanity and beneficence should not be limited to one people, and as citizens of the world we should consider all nations as our brothers. Nothing could be finer or more fortunate for mankind, if philosophy and patriotism could agree on this point. But what countless difficulties arise from the opposing interests of different peoples which cannot be reconciled. What are we to do, Madam, in these cases? How can we sacrifice the interests of our own ward, however uncouth he may be, for the sake of others? How can we bring about the general welfare in that lawsuit involving rights, claims, possessions, demanded by everyone? I confess, Madam, it is all algebra to me, and the problem is all the more difficult in that monarchs recognize no court from where an equitable and impartial judge could pronounce judgment on them; so that, invariably obsessed with their own rights, real or imaginary, they only yield in trifles and are inflexible on important points.

6 Voltaire on war

Published article by Voltaire; 1764

('War' in *Philosophical Dictionary*, R. Moland (ed) *Oeuvres complètes* Vol XIX (1879), Paris, pp. 319–21)

A genealogist proves to a monarch that he is the direct descendant of a count, whose parents made a family compact three or four hundred years ago with a house which no longer survives even in living memory. This house had some remote claims on a province whose last owner died of apoplexy. The monarch and his council see that his right to it is indisputable. This province, which is several hundred leagues away from his kingdom, protests that it does not know him, has no wish to be ruled by him; that if you wish to govern a people, you must at least have their consent. In vain: these arguments do not even reach the monarch whose rights are incontrovertible. He finds a large number of enthusiastic desperadoes. He dresses them in coarse blue uniforms with broad white binding on their hats,★ makes them turn right and left, and marches them off to glory . . .

What do humanity, decency, modesty, temperance, mildness, wisdom and piety mean to me, when half-a-pound of lead fired from six hundred feet away shatters my body, and I die in indescribable agony at the age of twenty amid five or six thousand dying men, and my eyes, as they open for the last time, see the town where I was born destroyed by sword and fire, and the last sounds to reach my ears are the cries of women and children dying beneath the ruins—all in the supposed interests of a man whom we do not know?

★ i.e. in Prussian uniform (see *Candide*, p. 22)

The first paragraph of document 6 is a biting parody of contemporary diplomatic practice. Frederick was openly cynical about his legal claims to Silesia and to Poland which, as he declared, having decided on annexation, 'the archives will furnish for me' (see section 8 documents 3 and 12).

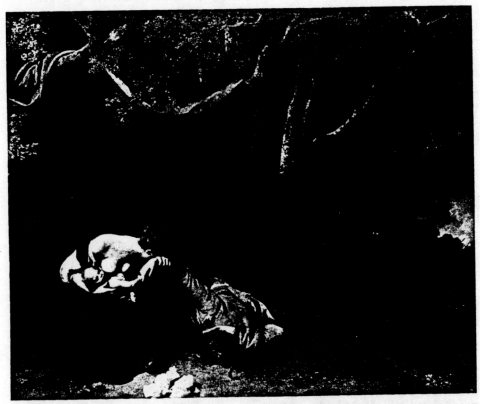

Figure 21   Joseph Wright of Derby, *The Dead Soldier*, 1789, oil on canvas, 101.5 × 127 cm (40 × 50 ins). 'Die quietly, can't you!' (Frederick the Great to a soldier mortally wounded). Photograph from Benedict Nicolson *Joseph Wright of Derby* (1968), Routledge and Kegan Paul, plate 281, p. 180.

7   *Frederick II on war*

Letter from Frederick II to Voltaire; 9 October 1773

(T. Besterman (ed) *Voltaire's Correspondence* Vol LXXXVI (1963), Geneva, pp. 49–50)

Personally, I renounce war, lest I be excommunicated by the *philosophes*. I read the article on war and shuddered. How can a ruler whose troops are dressed in coarse blue cloth and hats with white fringes, after making them turn right and left—how can he march them off to glory without deserving the honourable title of bandit chief, since he is followed by a mere pack of vagabonds, forced by need to become mercenary murderers and to follow under his leadership the honourable profession of highwayman? . . . There are, however, some just wars, though you will not admit that they exist; those necessitated by self-defence are undoubtedly of this kind.

8 Frederick II on war

Letter from Frederick II to Voltaire; 30 July 1774

(T. Besterman (ed) *Voltaire's Correspondence* Vol LXXXVIII (1963), Geneva, pp. 132–4)

As long as you fulminate with such forcefulness against that art which you call 'infernal', you will live, and I shall only believe that your end is near when you cease to insult the defenders of the State, those heroes who risk health, life and limb to protect their fellow-citizens. Since we would lose you if you did not launch these witticisms against soldiers, I allow you the exclusive privilege of amusing yourself at their expense. But imagine the enemy about to penetrate the outskirts of Ferney;* would you not regard as your Saviour the brave man who defended your lands and drove this enemy from your boundaries? . . .

But I do not know where I stray. Is it for me to suggest ideas to that solitary *philosophe*, who, from his study, furnishes the whole of Europe with ideas? I leave you to all those which your tireless imagination will suggest. If will doubtless tell you that it is as much use declaiming against snow and hail as against war; that these are inevitable evils; and that it is not worthy of a *philosophe* to take on lost causes. One asks a doctor to cure a fever, not to write a satire against it. If you have any cures, let us have them; if you have none, show sympathy for our misfortunes. Let us say like the angel Ituriel†: 'Although not everything in this world is good, everything is tolerable'; we must be content with our lot.

* Voltaire's estate
† In Voltaire's *Babouc* (1748)

Figure 22   E. F. Cunningham, *Death of Marshall Keith at Hochkirch*, 1758, oil on canvas 'Only the good get killed; my type always survives' (Frederick the Great). Berlin, Archiv für Kunst und Geschichte.

9 Frederick II on war

Letter from Frederick II to Voltaire; 16 February 1774

(T. Besterman (ed) *Voltaire's Correspondence* Vol LXXXVII (1963), Geneva, p. 77)

I would as soon declaim against scarlet fever as against war. The one will as little be stopped from making its ravages as the other from troubling the nations. There have been wars since the world began, and there will be wars long after you and I have paid our tribute to nature.

Would it be fair to describe Frederick's outlook on foreign policy as aggressive?

In the sense that Frederick's policy of military engagement twice plunged Europe into war (in 1740 and 1756), that it aimed at the seizure and retention of the Austrian province of Silesia, and that Prussian society and the economy was involved, directly or indirectly, in carrying out such a policy, it would be reasonable to describe it as aggressive.

For Frederick, however, offence and defence were inextricably mingled: all just wars were defensive; and all his wars and his military preoccupation, it could be argued (and he certainly argued), were ultimately defensive. For example, Frederick argued that his aim in invading Saxony in 1756 was defensive: to break out of the menacing encirclement of France, Austria and Russia, and to steal a march on them by a pre-emptive strike. His critics argue that his action was part of a deliberate war of aggression and conquest, pointing to his declared ambition to annex Saxony (see document 14). His apologists contend that though he hoped to compensate himself with new territories in the event of victory, such territorial aspirations were incidental to, not the cause of, the outbreak of war, which was the threat of anti-Prussian encirclement. (For the varying historical interpretations of Frederick's act, see Professor Sir Herbert Butterfield, 'The Reconstruction of an historical episode: the history of the enquiry into the origins of the Seven Years' War', in *Man on His Past*, 1955, Cambridge University Press, chapter 5.)

Another example is Frederick's policy after the Seven Years War. In 1763 Prussia emerged unbeaten and peace was re-established on the basis of the *status quo ante*. It had been, however, a very near-run thing, and Prussia had suffered enormous damage. Frederick faced the momentous decision whether to demobilize and reduce his forces to their pre-war or even their 1740 level. He chose instead to build them up still more and to maintain a huge peacetime standing army over 200 000 strong. This decision irrevocably established Prussia as a state permanently geared to military priorities. Some historians argue that Frederick could have disarmed in 1763 without serious risk. Prussia had survived the war and retained Silesia. The anti-Prussian coalition of France, Austria and Russia had disintegrated, and Russia was in fact acting in cooperation with Prussia. Frederick however, looked warily ahead, taking into account a constantly fluctuating situation, in which the potential long-term dangers to Prussia must be anticipated and could never be completely eliminated. When assured in 1763 that Austria had now genuinely renounced all hopes of regaining Silesia, he observed: 'A cat remains a cat, no matter what it does'.

For Frederick war was a fact of life, a 'regrettable necessity', inevitable against a background of continual competition and tension among the Great Powers. Pacifism or neutrality was folly, because Prussia would be left out of the spoils and/or herself be subject to attack and dismemberment. Preparedness for war and an aggressive posture were necessities for a vulnerable state on the make. As Frederick wrote in section 1 document 2, 'until it acquires far greater strength and better frontiers [Prussia] must be ruled by monarchs who are always alert, wary of their neighbours and ready to defend themselves from one day to the next against their enemies' designs'.

Eighteenth-century warfare

Eighteenth-century wars compare well with those of the seventeenth century in their far lower scale of casualties and material destruction. Seventeenth-century wars were often characterized by religious fanaticism, notably the Thirty Years War

(1618–48), which set Protestants and Catholics at each other's throats throughout Germany, with bands of mass marauders devastating the countryside, and horrible bloodbaths like the sack of Protestant Magdeburg by the Catholics in 1631, when the population of 30 000 was butchered and the city razed to the ground. Even where war-aims were political rather than religious, immense havoc was wreaked: in 1689, French troops deliberately demolished the cities of the Palatinate on the orders of Louis XIV. The most murderous battle of the eighteenth century was at Zorndorf in 1759 between the Prussians and Russians: here Frederick lost 20 000 men, though the extent of this loss was exceptional.[13]

In Frederick's day, wars were conducted according to fixed general principles, with limited objectives and limited means. The object was simply to put the enemy army out of action with the least possible loss to one's own side in men and money, not to carry out mass slaughter of civilians in the spirit of the crusades. Campaigns were fought seasonally by professional armies, whose freedom of action was severely restricted by economic and logistic considerations. Mobility, for example, was limited by the system of fixed supply depots: no army could safely venture more than five days' march from its depot. One of the most important moderating influences on war was the chronic threat of desertion. In the War of the Bavarian Succession between Prussia and Austria (1778–9), Frederick lost 3 500 men in battle and 16 000 by desertion. To have let loose his armies to forage or plunder at large, as in the seventeenth century, would have left him without an army to fight with! Hence the ferocious discipline operating in the Prussian army, of which the American historian Dorn writes: 'One gains the impression that the prime function of an officer was to prevent desertion; to fight the enemy was a secondary consideration' (compare section 4 p. 50).

Rulers were obsessed with the problem of maintaining large armies without disrupting the economy. The strains on the Prussian economy were particularly acute, for while the Austrian army was larger than Frederick's by one third, relative to the size of his population Frederick raised twice as many troops as Maria Theresa. This required all his organizational ingenuity: rather than let his army stand idle in peacetime, Frederick organized a rota system, under which 70 000 men were on leave for ten months of the year, working as agricultural labourers or building fortifications and canals; they returned to the colours in the summer for training, manoeuvres or mobilization in the event of war.

Frederick did not expect his troops to work up religious or pro-Prussian sentiments. Occasionally, in a tight corner (as at Kunersdorf in 1759), he did exploit their personal loyalty; and his great victories of Rossbach and Leuthen in 1757 were immensely popular in Prussia as Protestant triumphs over the Catholic armies of France and Austria (after Leuthen, his troops broke into the traditional hymn, 'Now thank we all our God', thereafter known as the 'Leuthen Chorale'). But Frederick deprecated such sentiments, regarding Prussian foreign policy as his own affair: the people should mind its own business and not bother which particular enemy he might see fit to attack in the interests of the State. His aims were territorial, not ideological: he attacked Austria for Silesia, not for Protestantism. National feeling as such was in its infancy; as Frederick's Minister of Justice, von Zedlitz put it, it was 'unnatural', the product of a 'diseased imagination'. There was in any case little room for it, with the presence in the army of sizeable non-Prussian contingents, such as the elite hussars (Hungarians and Poles) who by 1763 comprised 37 000 out of 140 000 men.

Frederick's Prussia, for all its 'militarism', was still far in spirit from the 'nation in arms', the mass levies of the coming Revolutionary and Napoleonic wars. The

[13] On the first day of the Battle of the Somme, 1 July 1916, there were 60 000 British casualties, including 20 000 killed. The battle continued until November, ending in stalemate.

eighteenth-century army was officered by nobles and manned by peasants.[14] Other civilians were not involved: 'neither the farmer, the manufacturer, the lawyer nor the scholar are diverted from their work'. At the height of the Seven Years War, the total percentage of the Prussian population drafted into the army was only 4.4 per cent[15] (compare radio programme 16, 'War and Peace in the Age of Reason').

10   Frederick II on eighteenth-century warfare

Letter from Frederick II to d'Alembert; 18 October 1770

(*Oeuvres de Frédéric le Grand* Vol XXIV (1848), Berlin, pp. 506–7)

After all, standing armies do not depopulate the countryside or impair industry. In any country, there can only be a certain number of farmers in proportion to the amount of land available for cultivation, and a certain number of workers in proportion to the size of the market; the rest would become beggars or highwaymen. Moreover, these large armies cause money to circulate, and spread equally across the provinces the revenues that the people supply to the government. The costly upkeep of these armies shortens the length of the wars; instead of thirty years, which they lasted over a century ago, rulers are obliged to end them far more quickly out of sheer insolvency. In our day, seven or eight annual campaigns at most exhaust the rulers' funds and make them amenable to peace negotiations.

It is also to be observed that these standing armies determine the conditions of war more definitely than was formerly the case. Today, at the first trumpet-blast, neither the farmer, the manufacturer, the lawyer, nor the scholar, are diverted from their work; they continue peacefully to pursue their normal occupations, leaving to the nation's defenders the task of avenging the nation. In former times, at the first alarm, troops were hastily levied, everyone became a soldier, the only thought was to repel the enemy; the fields lay fallow, the professions languished, and the soldiers, ill-paid, ill-kept, ill-disciplined, lived only by looting, and lived like bandits on the unhappy areas which were the scene of their depredations. All that has greatly changed; not that such disgraceful looting no longer exists in some armies; but the whole business of war bears no resemblance to the chaos that once prevailed.

D'Alembert takes a different view of contemporary war in his reply to Frederick of 30 November 1770:

> As for the example which he [Louis XIV] set to other rulers—of having enormous standing armies—one must begin by agreeing, however unjust one may be, that in today's conditions it is impossible for even the most enlightened rulers not to follow that example; it would be both contrary to reason and contrary to what they owe their subjects, to remain unarmed, while everyone around them is armed to the teeth. But I take the liberty of asking Your Majesty, would you not prefer, if your position did not compel you to do so, to have a hundred thousand more ploughmen, and a hundred thousand fewer soldiers, since the former bring you riches, while the latter cost you a great deal? I know that these large armies make the wars end sooner; but, Sire, these wars end only in exhaustion, and I think it is preferable, if one has a hundred thousand men to lose, to lose them in twenty or thirty years than in six or seven. I also agree that these large armies make it unnecessary to enrol troops at the first canon shot, as formerly. But, Sire, a prince who was only a warrior and not a philosopher, might surely abuse these large armies to make war more often and more irresponsibly, as Louis XIV indeed reproached himself on

[14] See Gibbon on the imperial Roman army. It was, he says, commanded 'by officers of a liberal birth and education; but the common soldiers, like the mercenary troops of modern Europe, were drawn from the meanest, and very frequently, from the most profligate, of mankind' (Course Anthology Vol 1, p. 191).

[15] In the First World War, 8 million Frenchmen, out of a population of some 40 million, were mobilized, i.e. 20 per cent.

his deathbed. Moreover, do not the expenses that these great armies demand
put Europe, even in peacetime, in a continual state of tension that does not
differ greatly from a continual state of war?

Oeuvres de Frédéric le Grand Vol XXIV (1848), Berlin, pp. 517–8

Foreign policy

11   *Frederick II on foreign policy*

Confidential memorandum intended for the use of his heir; 1752

('Testament politique' (1752) in G. B. Volz (ed) *Die Politischen Testamente Friedrichs des
Grossen* (1920), Berlin, p. 59)

Machiavelli says that a neutral Power surrounded by ambitious Powers would certainly
end by being destroyed. I am extremely sorry, but I must admit that Machiavelli is right.
Rulers must necessarily be ambitious; however, they must also be prudent, moderate and
enlightened by reason.

12   *Frederick II on foreign policy*

Published essay; 1777

('Essai sur les formes du gouvernement et sur les devoirs des souverains', *Oeuvres de
Frédéric le Grand* Vol IX (1848), Berlin, p. 202)

In the present European situation, when all rulers are armed, including some Great Powers,
capable of crushing weaker ones, prudence requires us to ally ourselves with other Powers,
whether to guarantee aid for ourselves in case of aggression; to deter our enemies from
their dangerous plans; or to support our allies in their just claims against potential
opponents. But this is not enough; we must be careful to keep a close check on our
neighbours, and especially on our enemies. Men are wicked, and we must be particularly
on our guard against being taken by surprise, because anything unexpected alarms and
disconcerts us; but this does not happen when we are prepared, however disagreeable the
awaited event. European politics are so deceptive that the most experienced man can be
taken in if he is not continually alert and on his guard.

13   *Frederick II on foreign policy*

Confidential memorandum intended for the use of his heir; 1752

('Testament politique' (1752), in G. B. Volz (ed) *Die Politischen Testamente Friedrichs des
Grossen* (1920), Berlin, pp. 51, 54, 75–6)

An experienced politician should always adopt a flexible approach, adjusted to the
circumstances in which he finds himself and the personalities with whom he has to deal.
It is a great mistake in foreign policy always to be aggressive, to seek to decide every issue
by force, or, conversely, always to use gentle and subtle methods. A man who follows
a uniform system is soon found out, and one must not be found out. If your method
becomes well-known, your enemies will correctly predict: 'If we do this, he will do so
and so'; while by changing and varying one's tactics, one baffles them and they make
wrong forecasts. But conduct as wise as this requires you to keep a permanent check on
yourself, and far from following your personal inclinations, you must pursue meticulously
the strategy which your real interests dictate. The main object is to hide your intentions,
and for that you must veil your character and only reveal a firmness moderated and
tempered by justice. I have endeavoured to deal with my enemies on this basis . . . Each
set of circumstances, each moment of time, each individual, requires a different approach.
If it is time to break off negotiations, it is advisable to declare your intentions firmly
and proudly; but it is no use for the storm to threaten, unless the lightning strikes
simultaneously. If you have many enemies, you must divide them, isolate the most
irreconcilable, attack him, negotiate with the rest, lull them to sleep, make separate peace,

even if you have to lose by it; and then once the principal enemy is beaten, there is always time to return and fall on the others, under the pretext that they have failed to carry out their engagements . . .

The foreign policy of weak rulers is a tissue of deceit; the foreign policy of great rulers consists of great prudence, dissimulation and love of glory. It is a grave mistake for a politician always to cheat; he is soon found out and despised. Clever minds reckon on a consistent approach; that is why you must change your tactics as much as possible, disguise them, and transform yourself into a Proteus, by seeming sometime quick, sometimes slow, sometimes aggressive and sometimes peaceable. This is the way to puzzle your enemies and make them wary of opposing you. Not only is it advisable to vary your methods; you must, above all, adjust them in accordance with events, circumstances, time, place and personalities. Never threaten your enemies; dogs who bark do not bite. Be polite in negotiations: tone down arrogant or insulting expressions; never exaggerate minor differences; do nothing out of personal pride and everything for the interest of the State. Be discreet, dissimulate your intentions. If the prestige of the State obliges you to draw the sword, let the thunder and lightening strike your enemies simultaneously. You should not violate treaties except for important reasons. You may do so (a) if you fear that your enemies are making a separate peace and you have the means and the time to forestall them; (b) if lack of money prevents you from continuing the war; or, finally, (c) if major advantages demand it. Acts of this kind can be carried out once, or at most, twice in a lifetime, but they are not expedients that one can resort to every day.

14   Frederick II on foreign policy

Confidential memorandum intended for the use of his heir; 1776

('Exposé du gouvernement prussien', in G. B. Volz (ed) *Die Politischen Testamente Friedrichs des Grossen* (1920), Berlin, pp. 241–2)

One of the first principles of foreign policy is to try to ally ourselves to whichever of our neighbours can inflict the most dangerous blows on the State. Hence we are allied to Russia,* because this leaves our back free on the East Prussian front and because as long as the alliance lasts, we need not fear an attack by Sweden on Pomerania.

Times may change, and a freakish turn of events may oblige us to make other arrangements, but we shall never find with other Powers the advantages equal to those we gain from Russia. The French troops are worthless, and the French usually help their allies only feebly; while the English, who are made for paying subsidies, sacrifice their allies to peace in order to further their own interests. I say nothing of the house of Austria, with whom it seems almost impossible that strong links can be formed. As for the question of what acquisitions would suit this Prussian monarchy, the Saxon states would without doubt be the most appropriate: they would round it off and form a barrier for it by the mountains separating Saxony and Bohemia, which would have to be fortified. It is hard to predict how this acquisition could take place. The surest way would be to conquer Bohemia and Moravia, and exchange them for Saxony; or it could be done by other exchanges or with the Rhineland possessions, including Jülich or Berg;† or by some other means. This acquisition is absolutely essential in order to give this State the solidarity it lacks. For as soon as we are at war, the enemy can march straight on Berlin without meeting the least opposition in his path. I say nothing, however, of our rights of succession in Ansbach,** Jülich and Berg, and Mecklenburg, because our claims there are well known, and we shall have to wait on events. As the State is not rich, we must above all avoid becoming involved in wars where there is nothing to gain; we exhaust ourselves to no purpose; and if a profitable occasion arose later, we would be unable to exploit it. All distant acquisitions are a burden upon the State. A village on the frontier is worth more than a principality sixty leagues away. One must strive to conceal as far as possible one's ambitions, and, if possible, to excite the envy of Europe against the Powers that

* From 1764 to 1780
† Prussia's claim to the Duchies of Jülich and Berg under Frederick-William I was first supported and then betrayed by Austria in 1739. Berg passed to Prussia in 1799; but both Duchies were then seized by Revolutionary France. They were eventually awarded to Prussia in the post-Napoleonic settlement of 1815
** Ansbach and Bayreuth, in Bavaria, passed to Prussia in 1799

one intends to attack. This can be done: the house of Austria, whose ambition is unconcealed, will attract in future the envy and jealousy of the Great Powers.†† Secrecy is an essential virtue in foreign policy as well as in the art of war.

†† Joseph II's scheme to annex Bavaria was foiled by Frederick's intervention in 1778–9 (War of the Bavarian Succession)

Exercise

Refer back to your notes on document 1, the *Anti-Machiavel*. Do you consider Frederick's views on foreign policy in documents 11–14 to be 'Machiavellian'?

Specimen answer and discussion

Yes, in the sense that where Prussian interests were concerned, even though he did not disguise the fact that such violations of morality were 'disagreeable necessities', he believed that the ends justified the means. Such was the philosophy of *raison d'état*, according to which the State is not subject to conventional moral restraints. On the contrary it can and must ignore the moral law if it is in its interest to do so. Frederick believed that foreign policy can be reduced to something like an exact science, by the study of history, a knowledge of human nature, the exploitation of others' weaknesses, the calculation of probabilities, and the careful use of deceit and fraud.

Frederick revealed his territorial ambitions so nakedly in his *Political Testament* of 1752 that in the 1880s Bismarck himself insisted on its partial suppression. It was published in full only in 1920. (See, for example, section 8 document 1.)

Frederick's critics link his writings, as evidence of his aggressive intentions, with the wars that followed, as evidence of his warmongering. There is, however, room for debate. It is possible to construe these documents as general long-term statements of *desirabilia* rather than as blueprints for immediate aggression. Frederick himself described them as 'chimerical projects' and 'political pipe dreams'. Note that he expresses a preference for peaceful, diplomatic conquest; war is a last resort. The fact that he was ultimately prepared to go to war in support of his claims surely suggests at least some degree of responsibility for the bloodshed and damage. But the same can be said of his contemporaries—Joseph II of Austria, or Catherine II of Russia. Was Frederick any worse in principle, or just more successful? (See section 8.)

It is also useful to remember that Frederick's wars lasted only a dozen years out of a reign of forty-six. Prussia's post-war recovery and economic expansion took place in a twenty-three-year-long interval of peace, though it is true that these years also saw the renewed build-up of the Prussian army. Ritter emphasizes Frederick's aims in the Seven Years War as limited to Prussia's survival, not her expansion. An important difference between Frederick and German statesmen of the age of nationalism is his indifference to territory as such: he would gladly drop his claims to the distant and indefensible Rhineland Duchies of Jülich and Berg in exchange for the strategically much more desirable Saxony—'a village on the frontier is worth more than a principality sixty leagues away'. No ruler in the later nationalistic age could afford to consider surrendering one acre of the 'sacred soil of the fatherland'.

The answer often seems to depend not only on one's interpretation of Frederick's policy but also on whether one takes a pro-Prussian view. The Austrian view was naturally anti-Prussian: Frederick's wars and the seizure of Silesia were won at Austria's expense, and his defiance of Austria's hegemony gravely undermined what was left of German unity in the Holy Roman Empire. Thus the pro-Austrian historian Klopp, in the 1860s, categorized Frederick's policy as pure aggression: 'This essence of the Hohenzollern state was the lust of conquest by long prepared and powerfully launched aggression in the field of foreign affairs and at home in the consequential military absolutism, both covered by falsehood and untruth.'

Frederick set Prussian Germans against Austrian Germans: 'He not only destroyed the Empire . . . he made peace among Germans impossible. He created dualism . . . as the beginning of a new era with the aggrandizement of the Hohenzollerns at any price and by any means as his goal' (quoted in G. P. Gooch, *Frederick the Great* (1947), Longman, p. 345).

8 The First Partition of Poland 1772

One of the acts of Frederick's foreign policy to be most severely condemned by liberal historians was his participation (together with Catherine II of Russia and Maria Theresa of Austria) in the first partition of Poland 1772, which stripped Poland of roughly one third of her territory and population and set the precedent for the remaining two partitions, which by 1795 eradicated Poland as a sovereign state. A cynical and brutal act, the first partition, it is suggested, reveals the true nature of Frederick's enlightened absolutism.

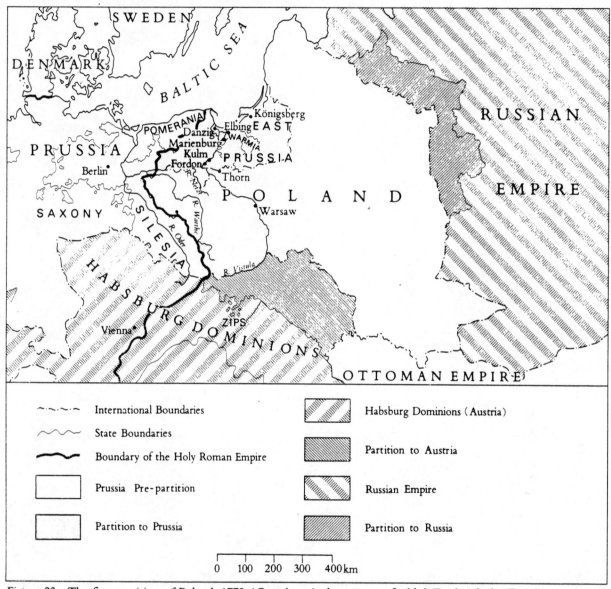

Figure 23 The first partition of Poland, 1772. 'Our share is the most profitable' (Frederick the Great).

Poland before partition

Eighteenth-century Poland was in a state of grave decline. A so-called 'crowned republic', she was an elective monarchy: on the death of each king a new monarch, with very limited powers, was elected by the Polish nobility, a group divided into factions and a prey to foreign intrigue and bribery. Constantly beset by civil war which was exacerbated by religious differences, Poland lacked natural frontiers and lay open to invasion; she had for her defence an army of only 13 000, and she was surrounded and dominated by the neighbouring absolute monarchies.

1 Frederick II on partition

Confidential memorandum intended for the use of his heir; 1752

('Testament politique' (1752), in G. B. Volz (ed) *Die Politischen Testamente Friedrichs des Grossen* (1920), Berlin, pp. 63–4)

After Saxony, the province that would suit us best would be Polish Prussia [West Prussia]. It separates East Prussia from Pomerania, and prevents us from sending support to the former because of the obstacle presented by the Vistula and the fear of possible Russian attacks via the Port of Danzig. This becomes clearer when you appreciate that East Prussia can only be attacked by the Muscovites; that if they make a descent on Danzig, they completely cut off the East Prussian army from our forces here, and that, if that army were forced to retreat, we would have to send out a considerable advance-party to cover its crossing of the Vistula.

I do not think that force of arms is the best way to add this province to the kingdom, and I would be tempted to say to you what Victor Amadeus, King of Sardinia, used to tell Charles Emmanuel: 'My son, we must eat up the Milanese like an artichoke, leaf by leaf'. Poland is an electoral kingdom; at the death of her kings, she is constantly troubled by factions. Here is where we must profit, and gain, by our neutrality, now a town, now another district, until everything is eaten up . . . Acquisitions made by the pen are always preferable to those made with the sword. One runs fewer risks that way, and does not exhaust one's purse or one's army.

Exercise

Comment on document 1 as an example of Frederick's methods.

Specimen answer and discussion

You may feel (as with section 7 document 14) that document 1 provides clear evidence of Frederick's long-hatched plans for aggression. Certainly it is true that he had designs on Polish territory. Note that the reasons given here are strategic—the isolation and vulnerability of East Prussia—fears that proved fully justified during the Seven Years War.

However, the idea of partitioning a state did not originate with Frederick: it was long since part of European practice; the partition of Poland had been mooted under Frederick-William I, and for thirty years Frederick was content to preserve Poland, weak but intact, as a buffer-state between Prussia and Russia. This situation was formalized in 1764 under an alliance between Frederick and Catherine, whereby it was agreed that the next king of Poland should be Stanislas Poniatowski (one of Catherine's former lovers). This suggests that document 1 constitutes another 'political pipe dream', a long-term aspiration dependent on contingencies rather than a concrete plan for a take-over of Poland. Frederick's actual policy did not change until 1771.

The politics of the partition

The crisis that led to partition arose from a disturbance to the balance of power caused by Russia's spectacular success in war against Turkey (1769–74). Russia's advance into the Balkans, regarded by Austria as a Habsburg sphere of influence, made imminent the prospect of a general European war, in which Austria would intervene against Russia on the side of Turkey, and Prussia, under the 1764 alliance with Russia, would be obliged to fight Austria over a Balkan quarrel in which Frederick had no interest. The possible method of a peaceful resolution of the crisis was suggested in 1770 by Austria's annexation of the district of Zips, a small enclave on her border with Poland, and Polish territory since 1412. This move prompted a radical reassessment by Catherine and Frederick of their policy towards Poland. In talks at St Petersburg with Frederick's brother, Prince Henry of Prussia,

Figure 24 Fedor Rokotov (1735–1808), *Catherine II*, oil on canvas, 81.2 × 68.5 cm (32 × 28 ins). 'Why should we not all take our share?' (Catherine the Great). Moscow, State Historical Museum.

Catherine raised the possibility of a tripartite partition, in which Austria and Russia would compromise over the Balkans at the expense of Poland, Frederick joining them in order to preserve Prussia's balance against Austria.

2   Prince Henry of Prussia on partition

Confidential dispatches from Prince Henry of Prussia to Frederick II; St Petersburg, 8 January 1771

(*Politische Correspondenz Friedrichs des Grossen* Vol XXX (1905), Berlin, pp. 406–7)

In the evening I called on the Empress [Catherine II], who mentioned in a joking vein how the Austrians had occupied two districts in Poland, and had erected the imperial emblems along the frontiers of these districts. 'But why should we not all take our share?' she added. I replied that while you, my dearest brother, had set up a cordon★ in Poland, you had not occupied any districts. 'But why not?' said the Empress, laughing. A moment later, Count Chernyshov† approached me and took up the same subject, adding: 'Why not occupy the bishopric of Warmia? After all, everyone should have something!' Although this was only a light-hearted conversation, it is certain that the topic was not raised for no reason.

★ As a measure to prevent the spread of the plague, then raging in Poland
† Russian Minister of War, advocate of a partition in Poland

3   Frederick II on partition

Confidential dispatches from Frederick II to Count Solms★; 20 February 1771

(*Politische Correspondenz Friedrichs des Grossen* Vol XXX (1905), Berlin, pp. 457–8)

So if we examine the realities of the situation, the question is no longer one of maintaining Poland intact, since the Austrians want to dismember a part of it, but of preventing this dismemberment from upsetting that balance of power between the House of Austria and my own, the maintenance of which is so important to me and of such concern to the Russian court too. Now I see no other way of ensuring the maintenance of this balance than to follow the example set by the Court of Vienna, to enforce, as it is doing, some old claims which the archives will furnish for me, and to take possession of some small Polish province, with a view to giving it back if the Austrians desist from their enterprise, or to keeping it if they wish to enforce their so-called claims.

* Prussian Ambassador at St Petersburg

4   *Frederick II on partition*

Confidential dispatches from Frederick II to Count Solms; 14 June 1771

(F. de Smitt *Frédéric, Catherine et le partage de la Pologne, d'après des documents authentiques* Part II (1861), Paris, pp. 23–4)

I think, to start with what concerns me, we might propose that we be given possession of Pomerelia, with the exception of Danzig, and, as compensation for that town, the districts of Kulm and Marienburg; or, if this proposal seems too difficult, then instead of Pomerelia—Warmia, Elbing, Marienburg and Kulm. However, the first proposal will always be the most advantageous, if you can bring it off, because it gives me direct communication with East Prussia, from which, otherwise, I remain permanently cut off by Poland. I trust to your zeal and skill to bring it off. As for the steps involved in this acquisition, I think it is absolutely essential that there should be a convention between the two courts [of Prussia and Russia] concerning their mutual acquisitions, and in this connection you will find the enclosed plan. I am not concerned with the share which Russia has in mind for herself, and I have deliberately given her *carte blanche* to arrange this according to her interests and her desires.

5   *Secret convention between Russia and Prussia*

Secret treaty; 17 February 1772

(F. de Smitt *Frédéric II, Catherine et le partage de la Pologne*, Part II (1861), Paris, pp. 75–7)

His Majesty the King of Prussia . . . will take possession of the whole of Pomerelia (excluding the city of Danzig and its territory) and the district of Great Poland on this side of the Netze, following this river from the frontier of the New Mark to the Vistula, near Fordon and Solitz, so that the Netze shall form the frontier of the states of His Majesty the King of Prussia, and that this river shall belong entirely to him; and his aforesaid Majesty, not wishing to enforce his other claims to several other districts in Poland bordering Silesia and East Prussia, which he could justly claim, and waiving at the same time any claim to the city of Danzig and its territory; . . . his Majesty will take by way of compensation the rest of Polish Prussia, namely the palatinate of Marienburg, including the town of Elbing, the bishopric of Warmia and the palatinate of Kulm, with the sole exception of the town of Thorn, which town shall be maintained together with all its territory under the rule of the Republic of Poland.

In order not to be outbid, Austria was forced to make larger claims on Poland proportionate to those of Prussia and Russia, despite the qualms of the conscience-stricken Maria Theresa. 'She wept, but she took', observed Frederick, adding that the more she wept, the more she took.

6   *Frederick II on partition*

Confidential dispatches from Frederick II to Count Solms; 22 April 1772

(F. de Smitt *Frédéric II, Catherine et le partage de la Pologne* Part II (1861), Paris, pp. 112–3)

The most important thing at the moment is to ascertain the share that the court of Vienna is demanding from Poland. According to its latest proposals, it is demanding a very large share indeed, greatly exceeding that equality of shares originally stipulated in the agreement concluded between us . . . If the court of Vienna obtains all its demands, there will no longer be any balance between our acquisitions, and the balance of power will lean even further in Austria's favour. As it is, she is already now more powerful than I. In order to restore a proper balance, it will be absolutely necessary to make our shares★ proportionately larger. However . . . I flatter myself that everything can still be amicably settled at St Petersburg.

★ i.e. those of Prussia and Russia

Figure 25   The situation in Poland in 1773, with Frederick the Great at the extreme right; engraving. 'A very good bargain' (Frederick the Great). Berlin, Staatsbibliothek Preussischer Kulturbesitz, Bildarchiv.

7   Frederick II on partition

Confidential dispatches from Frederick II to Prince Henry of Prussia; 18 June 1772

(*Oeuvres de Frédéric le Grand* Vol XXVI (1855), Berlin, p. 359)

I have seen a large part of the portion which falls to us as a result of the partition. Our share is the most profitable as far as trade is concerned. We gain control over all of Poland's imports and exports, which is a major asset; and the greatest advantage of all is that, once in control of the wheat trade, we shall never at any time be exposed to famine in that province. The population of this acquisition is as much as 600 000, and we shall soon be able to raise it to 700 000; especially since all the Dissidents★ in Poland will seek asylum there. That, my dear brother, is what we must work for, for the first object in any state is to increase its population in proportion as the land is capable of feeding its inhabitants.

★ The oppressed Protestant minorities

Outline and explain Frederick's reaction to the Austrian annexation of Zips
(documents 3–7).

The Austrian move prompted a reappraisal by Frederick of his policy towards
Poland. The Austrian annexation threatened to disturb the balance of power in the
Polish area; at the same time it suggested a way for all three Powers involved to
avoid the threat of war over the Balkans. Since neither Catherine nor Frederick was
prepared to acquiesce in a unilateral increase in Austrian territory (which would
have threatened Prussia's hold on Silesia), the only solution lay in a similar move
on their parts. 'I see no other way', as Frederick observed, 'of ensuring the
maintenance of this balance than to follow the example set by the Court of Vienna.'
By extending their own borders at Poland's expense, they would restore the balance
of power between them in the region and bring to Prussia territory of unique
strategic and (as he now noted) economic importance.

Finis Poloniae

Vigorous negotiations followed between Catherine and Frederick and the extent of
their respective shares was agreed in February 1772. In their public documents,
issued simultaneously with their military intervention in the summer of 1772, the
occupying Powers presented the partition

1   as a peace-saving operation for the restoration of order in Poland, where political
anarchy certainly provided a plausible excuse for intervention (though the various
warring factions were backed by Russia and Russia in order to create an
increasingly chaotic internal situation) and

2   as the vindication of territorial claims, which Frederick, at least, admitted readily
enough, were spurious.

They also insisted on the formal renunciation of her lost provinces by the rump
Poland, on which they also imposed 'a political existence more in accordance with
their interests as neighbouring countries', legitimizing their further right to
intervene and pointing irresistibly to Poland's subsequent disappearance as a
sovereign state. Documents 8 and 10 bring out Frederick's extreme cynicism in his
public pronouncements and his behind-the-scenes manoeuvering over the partition.

8   Treaty of partition between Russia and Prussia

Public document, treaty; 5 August 1772

(K. Lutostanski (ed) *Recueil des actes diplomatiques, traités et documents concernant la Pologne*,
Vol I: *Les partages de la Pologne et la lutte pour l'indépendance* (1918), Paris, pp. 40–41)

In the name of the Most Holy Trinity

The spirit of faction, the troubles and the civil war by which the kingdom of Poland has
for so many years been disturbed, and the anarchy which daily gains new strength there,
to the point of destroying all regular governmental authority, giving rise to just fears of
seeing the total collapse of the state, troubling the relations of all its neighbours, disturbing
the harmony existing between them and igniting a general war; . . . And at the same time,
the neighbouring Powers of the Republic, possessing claims and rights as old as they are
legitimate, which they have never been able to enforce and which they stand to lose
irretrievably unless they take steps to protect and enforce them, together with the
restoration of law and order within this Republic, as well as determining for it a political
existence more in accordance with their interests as neighbouring countries . . .

9 The King of Poland on partition

Letter from Poniatowski to Mme Geoffrin*; 19 September 1772

(C. de Mouy (ed) *Correspondance inédite du roi Stanislas Poniatowski et de Madame Geoffrin* (1875), Paris, pp. 433–4)

Since you would rather have sad letters from me than none at all, I reply to your letter of 27 August, by informing you that the storm that has been brooding over my head for six months, has just broken. On the thirteenth of this month, the King of Prussia occupied the whole of Polish Prussia, apart from the cities of Danzig and Thorn. Yesterday his minister and the Russian minister presented my ministers with a memorandum informing me of the seizure by their courts of a part of my kingdom, the titles to which they intend to make known in due course. In the same document, they inform me that the court of Vienna is to do likewise, by common agreement with them. The Austrian minister is not yet here, but is due today or tomorrow. Meanwhile, the three armies, Russian, Prussian and Austrian, and especially the second, are bleeding the country white, both inside and beyond the boundaries of the provinces which they claim to be appropriating. Poland is now maintaining over a hundred thousand foreign troops, and our own few remaining troops, numbering less than ten thousand, are at this moment under attack.

In the territory being taken from Poland, I lose for my part two-thirds of my revenue; and in the territory which they claim to leave me, the inhabitants often live at their mercy.

* Patroness of d'Alembert and Diderot, she held a well-known *salon* attended by the *philosophes*.

10 Frederick II on the partition

Confidential dispatches from Frederick II to Count Solms; 11 November 1772

(F. de Smitt *Frédéric, Catherine et le partage de la Pologne* Part II (1861), Paris, pp. 182–3)

Having given further thought as to how to obtain from the King and the Republic of Poland the surrender of the provinces of which the three Courts have taken possession, I am all the more in favour of the idea that I communicated to you in my last orders, namely, that we must act with the greatest firmness towards these folk, and even advance our troops still further into the kingdom. According to my latest letters from Warsaw, as a result of the last meeting of the Senate, they have started sending letters to all the European Powers, asking for their intervention and their aid against any implementation of our treaty of partition. They have even sent one to Her Majesty the Empress of Russia, as well as to the Empress-Queen* and myself . . . And although it appears from these letters that they have given up their original idea of summoning every last man and dying with their weapons in their hands, rather than subscribing to what they call Poland's disgrace, I do not think that we shall ever obtain their signature of surrender unless we compel them by force. Prince Kaunitz† is of the same opinion over this, and they tell me from Vienna that his advice is that, instead of uselessly dispensing money in that kingdom to make the nation more amenable, the three Courts should rather announce in reply that it was only out of moderation that they confined themselves to taking the districts which each of them occupies as compensation for their respective claims in Poland; and that, in view of the aversion shown at Warsaw towards recognizing the just motives that prompted our courts to act in this way, they have felt obliged to take other measures, and that they will not fail to enforce their claims in full. This minister would also like all our respective troops to advance further into the kingdom.

* Maria Theresa
† Austrian Chancellor

11 Frederick II on the partition

Letter from Frederick II to Voltaire; 9 October 1773

(T. Besterman (ed) *Voltaire's Correspondence* Vol LXXXVI (1963), Geneva, p. 49)

I know that Europe in general thinks that the partition of Poland is a result of political intrigues attributed to me. But nothing could be further from the truth. After having proposed in vain various different compromises, it was essential to resort to this partition as the only way of avoiding general war. Appearances are deceptive, and the public judges only by appearances. What I tell you is as true as Euclid's forty-eighth theorem.

12 Frederick II on the partition

Published memoirs; 1775

('Mémoires depuis la paix de Hubertusbourg jusqu'à la fin du partage de la Pologne', *Oeuvres de Frédéric le Grand* Vol VI (1847), Berlin, pp. 46–7)

The King based his claims to Pomerelia and part of Poland north of the Netze, on the fact that these provinces, which were once annexed to Pomerania, had been torn from it by the Poles. He claimed the town of Elbing by virtue of loans of money and silver which his ancestors had advanced to the Republic on the security of that town. The bishoprics of Warmia and the palatinates of Marienburg and Kulm were claimed as compensation for the city of Danzig, the capital of Pomerelia, which is to remain independent. We are not prepared to justify the validity of these claims, nor those of the Russians, still less those of the Austrians. It required an extraordinary combination of circumstances to bring about agreement for this partition, and it was done in order to avoid a general war.

Such was the outcome of these many negotiations, which demanded patience, firmness and skill. We succeeded on this occasion in saving Europe from a general war that was close to breaking out. Interests as contrary as those of the Russians and the Austrians were hard to reconcile. To indemnify the Russians for their conquests, which the Austrians wished them to restore to the Porte [Turkey], there was no other way than to assign to them territory in Poland. The Empress-Queen had set the example, by sending her troops to occupy the principality of Zips; and in order that the balance should somehow be maintained between the northern Powers, it was absolutely essential for the King to take part in the partition. This is the first example in history of a partition peacefully coordinated and carried out by three Powers. Without the particular circumstances in which Europe then found itself, the most skilful statesmen would have failed: everything depends on time and circumstances.

13 Maria Theresa on the partition

Letter from Maria Theresa to the Archduke Ferdinand;★ 17 September 1772

(A. von Arneth (ed) *Briefe der Kaiserin Maria Theresia an Ihre Kinder und Freunde* Vol I (1881), Vienna, p. 151)

That wretched partition of Poland . . . has taken ten years off my life. You will read the whole miserable story of that affair. How many times I said no! It was only the repeated Turkish setbacks, the lack of hope of help from France or England, and the prospect of my being isolated and exposed to a war against the Russians and Prussians, the poverty, famine and mortality here at home—it was this alone that forced me to join in that wretched scheme, which is a blot on my entire reign. May it be God's will that I shall not have to answer too much for it in the next world. I admit, I shall never be done with this subject, it is so much on my mind and vexes me and poisons my days, which are sad enough in any case. I must stop short so as not to vex myself unduly about it and fall into the blackest depression.

★ Her younger son

14 Vergennes on the partition

Memorandum by Vergennes★; 1774

(Adapted from 'Exposé sur la situation politique de la France' (1774) in F. Piggot and

★ French Foreign Minister

G. W. T. Omond (eds) *Documentary History of the Armed Neutralities, 1780 and 1800* (1919), University of London Press, pp. 44–5)

Posterity will find it hard to believe what an indignant Europe sees with astonishment: three Powers, with different and opposing interests, joining together in a blatant outrage; by brute force stripping of its richest domains an innocent state, against which they have no title apart from its weakness and inability to resist the greed of its invaders. If force is a right, if expediency is a title, how safe will states be henceforth? If immemorial possession and solemn treaties laying down respective boundaries no longer serve as a break on ambition, how can one guarantee against surprise-attack and invasion? If political brigandage is to continue, peace will soon be no more than a career open to faithlessness and treachery. It is less than a century ago that Europe was seen to band together and flood the world with blood in order to avenge the seizure of a few villages.† Now Austria, Russia and Prussia unite to dismember a great kingdom and divide its provinces among themselves; the rest of Europe sees it, remains silent and tolerates it. England, once so zealous and ardent for the maintenance of the Balance of Power, does not even seem to notice this *démarche*, which should really alarm it . . . For nearly two centuries, the Great Powers directed all their aims and sacrificed all their resources, to the point of exhaustion, in order to prevent any one of them from becoming preponderant. A new situation is replacing this system of general balance: three Powers strive to establish a particular balance, they create it by means of the equality of their usurpations, and this is how they make the balance of power lean heavily in their favour.

† i.e. the European coalitions against the expansionism of Louis XIV

Exercise===

Consider the following judgment by the Prussian historian, Otto Hintze, published during the First World War in 1915:

> The First Partition of Poland in 1772 was a masterpiece of Frederician diplomacy. Not only was the grave danger of a major war averted, but Prussia acquired long-coveted West Prussia . . . This territory was an ancient German colonial sphere, and now peaceful methods had restored it to rule by a German state. Since it had suffered tremendous decline in Polish hands, it became the object of special concern on the King's part. Whatever sort of injustice may have been committed against Poland was thus more than made up. . . . The King called his new possession an offshoot of anarchy. He compared it with Canada and with the Iroquois Indians. Order and a higher form of civilization became possible only with the introduction of Prussian rule.
>
> O. Hintze, *Die Hohenzollern und Ihr Werk* (1915), Berlin, pp. 389–90; translated by T. Barker in *Frederick the Great and the making of Prussia*, European Problem Studies (1972) pp. 42–3

Summarize the pros and cons of this argument.

Specimen answer and discussion===========================

It can certainly be agreed that the partition was 'a masterpiece of Frederician diplomacy', without forgetting the 'extraordinary combination of circumstances', without which, as Frederick himself modestly admitted, 'the most skilful statesmen would have failed' (document 12). The partition was a triumph of the policy of opportunism which Frederick expressed in section 1, document 2: 'We should not believe that we can shape events; but when they present themselves, we must seize them in order to exploit them.'

It is almost certainly true that a European war was averted by the partition; and Frederick was, I think, perfectly sincere in maintaining that that was its primary purpose, even if it also brought useful dividends in the shape of West Prussia. However, Hintze's implied defence of the partition on the grounds that West Prussia was 'an ancient German colonial sphere' is rejected by Frederick himself in his frank admission that he was 'not prepared to justify the validity of those claims'.

It is also correct that underdeveloped West Prussia now enjoyed the benefits of Prussian rule and Frederick's special attention. It should be remembered that to cosmopolitan contemporaries like Voltaire, the partition was far less of an outrage to *national* sentiment than it was to become in the nineteenth century, though it was recognized as a gross violation of state sovereignty and a cynical extension of the doctrine of the balance of power (documents 13–14).

Exercise

Now consider the 'liberal' view of the English historians, Marriot and Robertson, whose work was also published in 1915, and note how far you agree:

> Frederick's action has been defended, firstly, because Poland was a dying kingdom, which the surgery of partition restored to a new life in the march of Prussian civilization and progress; secondly, because he had at length recovered the whole territory ruled by the Teutonic Order, and only took back what had been once germanized by German blood and sweat; thirdly, because he reorganized his acquisition and with marvellous labour conferred on it by the blessings of an enlightened autocracy and an efficient administration; fourthly, because if he had not forestalled Catherine and Joseph [son of, and co-ruler with, Maria Theresa], they would have made the Partition, and he would have obtained nothing; fifthly, because the geographical, political and military needs of Prussia required that the gap between East Prussia and Prussian Pomerania should be filled in. . . . These arguments are simply embroidered variants of the central doctrine that ends justify means and that reason of state and the law of dynastic needs, backed by bayonets, are superior to all other considerations. They would apply to and justify any and every aggressive conquest. Frederick paved the way to robbery by an iniquitous agreement with Catherine that Poland should remain decadent, anarchic and unreformed. His diplomacy was throughout a tissue of fraud and deceit, and the consummation of his designs was only effected by sheer force on an unwilling victim. The partition was, and remains, a crime; it provided an odious precedent for the subsequent extinction of the Polish kingdom . . .; and it taught a world on the eve of revolution that enlightened monarchs differed from the footpad only in the magnitude of their greed, the scale of their operations and the philosophical hypocrisy with which they sought to cover naked aggression.

> J. A. Marriot and C. G. Robertson, *The Evolution of Prussia* (revised edition 1968), Oxford University Press, pp. 152–3

Specimen answer and discussion

These arguments are essentially a repetition of the points made by the French minister, Vergennes, in document 14. From the moral point of view, it seems to me they are unanswerable.

However, without denying this view of the partition as 'a crime', it seems to me important in order to understand (though not necessarily to condone) it to see it in context.

The underlying cause of the partition was the presence of a power-vacuum in eastern Europe caused by the chronic weakness of the existing Polish state, overextended, without defensible frontiers, unarmed, lacking social and political cohesion. In theory, Poland existed as an independent state, by virtue of international law; in fact her existence in the eighteenth century depended on the consent of her more powerful neighbours, Prussia, Russia and Austria. Once that consent was withdrawn, whatever fresh solution to the Polish problem was found would likewise depend on her neighbours. The immediate occasion for partition was the decline of Turkish power, when partition emerged as a means of

1   localizing international conflict and preventing it from exploding in a general European war and

2   peacefully restoring the balance of power and reconciling the conflicting interests of the Great Powers concerned.

Partition was thus a natural corollary of the system of the balance of power. The recognition of these facts of international life, and their adroit manipulation by the rulers, suggests a clear-headed pragmatism rather than exceptional wickedness. Certainly Frederick was no worse than his 'accomplices', each of whom took far bigger slices of Polish territory than Frederick. 'I hope that posterity', he wrote, 'will distinguish the philosopher in me from the ruler, the man of honour from the politician. It is very difficult to maintain integrity and good faith if one is embroiled in the stormy waters of European politics.'

9 Enlightenment and Progress

Faith in Progress is traditionally held to be one hallmark of the Enlightenment. We have seen a confident expression of this in Gibbon's chapter XXXVIII and in d'Alembert's *Preliminary Discourse*. But it is clear that considerable reservations about Progress were entertained by many *philosophes*, particularly after the Seven Years War. They tended to argue the possibility rather than the inevitability of progress (compare Stuart Brown on d'Alembert and 'Enlightenment', Units 13–14 pp. 60–76). Against this background, Frederick's somewhat acerbic remarks suggest that he was a man of his age in this respect, rather than an isolated misanthrope.

1 Frederick II on Progress

Letter from Frederick II to Voltaire; 11 April 1759

(T. Besterman (ed) *Voltaire's Correspondence* Vol XXXVI (1958), Geneva, p. 22)

I think people have forgotten in this war [the Seven Years War] the meaning of good manners and decency. The most civilized nations are waging war like wild animals. I am ashamed of humanity; I blush for the century. Let us admit the truth: the arts and philosophy extend only to the few; the vast mass, the common people and the bulk of the nobility, remain what nature has made them, that is to say savage beasts.

2 Frederick II on Progress

Letter from Frederick II to Voltaire; 2 July 1759

(T. Besterman (ed) *Voltaire's Correspondence* Vol XXXVI (1958), Geneva, pp. 204–5)

The abominable enterprise of Damiens,* the cruel assassination attempt against the King of Portugal, are the sort of outrages that are committed in peace and war alike; they are the results of the folly and blindness of an absurd fanaticism. Despite the schools of philosophy, man will remain the most vicious animal in the universe; superstition, interest, vengeance, treason, ingratitude, will until the end of time produce bloody and tragic scenes, because we are ruled by passion, and very seldom by reason. There will always be wars, trials, devastation, plagues, earthquakes, bankruptcies. These form the subject-matter of all the history-books in the world. I suppose, since that is how things are, that it must be necessary. Professor Pangloss† will tell you why. As for myself, I, who have not the honour of a doctorate, I confess my ignorance to you. I think, however, that if a beneficent being created the universe, he would have made us happier than we are.

* He attempted to assassinate Louis XV in 1757
† Pangloss preached the philosophy of Optimism in Voltaire's *Candide*

Rousseau

Rousseau, persecuted by church and state in France and spurned by the *philosophes* (particularly after his *Discourse on the Arts and Sciences, Discourse on Inequality* and in 1762 his controversial novel on education, *Emile*), fled to Geneva, but fell foul of the Swiss authorities too. Frederick, while sharing the *philosophes'* antipathy to Rousseau's ideas (compare section 6, document 4) granted him asylum in the territory of Neuchâtel, a small Prussian enclave in Switzerland. Here he spent eighteen months (1762–3) under the protection of the Governor, George Keith, Earl Marischal of Scotland, a former Jacobite, at that time in the Prussian service and an erudite and cultivated man, one of the few colleagues whom Frederick genuinely respected.

3　Frederick II on Rousseau

Letter from Frederick II to George Keith, Earl Marischal; 1 September 1762

(*Oeuvres de Frédéric le Grand* Vol XX (1852), Berlin, pp. 288–90)

Your letter, my dear Keith, about Rousseau of Geneva, gave me great pleasure. I see that we think alike: we must assist that poor, wretched fellow, whose only sin is in holding odd opinions which he thinks valid. I shall have a hundred crowns sent to you; please arrange to give him as many as his needs require. I think if one gives him things, he will accept them more readily than money. If we were not at war, if we were not ruined, I would have a hermitage with a garden built for him, where he could live as he believed our ancestors lived. I confess that my ideas are as far from his as the finite is from the infinite; he will never persuade me to browse on the grass and walk on all fours. It is true that all that asiatic luxury, that refined style of good living, voluptuousness and softness, is not essential for our preservation, and that we could live with more simplicity and frugality than we do. But why renounce the pleasures of life when we can enjoy them? The true philosophy, it seems to me, is that which contents itself with condemning the abuse, without forbidding the use; we should learn to do without everything, while renouncing nothing. I must say that many of the modern philosophers displease me by the paradoxes they advance. They wish to proclaim new truths, and they come out with errors which are an insult to common sense. I stick to Locke, to my friend Lucretius, to my good old Emperor Marcus Aurelius; those men have told us all we can know (apart from Epicurus' physics),★ and all that can make us moderate, virtuous and wise. After that, it is absurd to tell us that we are all equal, and that consequently we must live like savages, without laws, society or civilization, that the fine arts have harmed morals, and other similarly untenable paradoxes. I think that your friend Rousseau missed his vocation: he was certainly born to become a famous cenobite, a Desert Father, famous for his austerities and mortifications, a Stylite. He would have performed miracles, he would have become a saint, and he would have added to the enormous list of martyrs; but today, he will merely be regarded as an eccentric philosopher, who is reviving after two thousand years the beliefs of Diogenes.† It is not worth grazing on the grass, or having rows with all his contemporary philosophers, for this.

★ The Greek philosopher Epicurus held that the universe was made up of countless atoms in motion. In contrast to the Stoics, he taught that there was no directing providence and that the gods were not concerned with human affairs. Epicurus' theory was the theme of the Roman poet Lucretius in his poem, *On the Nature of the Universe*
† Greek 'cynic' philosopher, who despised worldly goods and lived in a tub

Figure 26　Caryatids by F. C. Glume, at Sans-Souci. 'Why renounce the pleasures of life when we can enjoy them?' (Frederick the Great). Photograph by Paul Kafno.

4   Frederick II on Progress

Letter from Frederick II to Voltaire; *c* 20 August 1766

(T. Besterman (ed) *Voltaire's Correspondence* Vol LXII (1961), Geneva, pp. 131–2)

Even among the nations most refined by literature, we still see the remains of their former savage manners. It is very difficult to make the human race good and to tame this beast, the wildest of all. I am confirmed in my feeling that opinions have only a slender influence on men's actions; for I see that everywhere their passions prevail over their reason. Let us suppose, however, that you actually succeeded in bringing about a revolution in men's way of thinking; the sect that you would form would hardly be numerous, because it would be necessary to be a thinking person in order to belong to it, and few people are capable of strict, logical reasoning. And what about all those who have a vested interest in opposing the rays of light that reveal their baseness? What about those rulers who have been taught that their reign is only secure as long as the people follow religion? What about the populace, whose only reasoning lies in its prejudices, and which hates novelties in general?

Figure 27   The masks of Comedy and Tragedy; stucco at Sans-Souci by J. M. Merck and K. J. Sartori. 'Piss well and be cheerful: that is the best one can do in this world' (Frederick the Great). Photograph by Paul Kafno.

5   Frederick II on Progress

Letter from Frederick II to Voltaire; 29 September 1775

(T. Besterman (ed) *Voltaire's Correspondence* Vol XCII (1964), Geneva, p. 43)

You approve, I believe, of the constitution of Pennsylvania as it exists at present. It has only been in existence a century; in another five or six years you will no longer recognize it, so much is instability one of the permanent laws of this world.* Let philosophers establish the wisest form of government, it will suffer the same fate. Have these same philosophers always been free from error? Have they too not produced some of their own? Witness the 'substantial forms' of Aristotle, the mumbo-jumbo of Plato, the 'vortices' of Descartes, the 'monads' of Leibniz.† What should I say of the paradoxes with which

* The 1682 constitution of the Quaker colony of Pennsylvania guaranteed freedom of religion. Quaker predominance in government was ended by the revolutionary constitution of 1776
† Frederick refers to the various theories concerning the essence of matter produced by these philosophers

Rousseau has entertained Europe, if indeed one can include among the *philosophes* the man who has deranged the minds of some good fathers to the point of bringing up their children according to the principles of *Emile*! From all these examples it is clear that despite their good intentions and the trouble they take, men will never attain perfection, in whatever field it may be.

6 Frederick II on Progress

Letter from Frederick II to d'Alembert; 18 May 1782

(*Oeuvres de Frédéric le Grand* Vol XXV (1854), Berlin, pp. 225–6)

For all the love we have for the good of humanity, no legislator, no philosopher will change the nature of things. Our species probably must have always been as we know it now, a strange mixture of good and bad. Education and study may enlarge our sphere of knowledge, a good government may produce some hypocrites, wearing the mask of virtue; but never will men succeed in changing our character. I regard man as a clockwork machine subject to the springs which drive it; and what people call reason or wisdom is merely the fruit of experience, which influences the fear or the hope which determines our actions. This, my dear d'Alembert, is rather humiliating for our pride, but unfortunately it is only too true.

7 Frederick II on the philosopher-prince

Letter from Frederick II to Electress Maria Antonia of Saxony; 16 April 1766

(*Oeuvres de Frédéric le Grand* Vol XXIV (1854), Berlin, p. 112)

I am not presenting you, Madam, with a picture of what ought to be, but of what is, and what everyday experience brings forcibly to the notice of those who pay attention to the ways of the world. Plato was a great philosopher; he drew up the laws of his *Republic* in his study, without consulting experience, without consulting human nature or practical possibilities; and his *Republic* is only a political dream which could never be brought about. One can call it the Utopia of a virtuous man. From this, Madam, I conclude that many things seem easy on reflection in one's study which cannot be put into practice, not for lack of goodwill, but because of practical, unforeseeable difficulties which reveal themselves on closer examination.

Exercise ══════════════════════════════════════

How far do you feel that Frederick was really influenced by Enlightenment ideas?

Discussion ═════════════════════════════════════

Some critics discount Enlightenment ideas as a significant element in Frederick's outlook and policy, assessing them as mere window-dressing—'either filling idle hours or providing a hypocritical mask for brutally aggressive policies' (Paret). Others concede that Frederick was steeped in Enlightenment ideas, but argue that this had no practical effect on his rule.

As Professor Horn puts it: 'Voltaire had no influence upon the King of Prussia's statecraft'. He goes on:

> It is hard to attribute any specific influence on Frederick's ideas to Voltaire. Religious toleration, abolition of torture and economic development were already part of his mental furniture. They were part of the *Zeitgeist*:[16] Frederick did not owe them to Voltaire or the *philosophes*, but it pleased him to find that his ideas coincided so far with theirs that his actions could be justified in accordance with most enlightened social theories of the day.
>
> D. B. Horn *Frederick the Great and the Rise of Prussia* (Second edition 1967), English University Press, p. 55

[16] Spirit of the age

Frederick's ideas, like most people's, were formed in early life; and his were rooted in the Roman classics and the ideas of the seventeenth and first half of the eighteenth century—in Plutarch, Tacitus and Marcus Aurelius, in Locke, Bayle and Voltaire, in scepticism, materialism, scientific progress, not in the more revolutionary ideas of the second half of the eighteenth century. He did not take to the books that came out after the Seven Years War. He not only totally rejected Rousseau's ideas—most of the *philosophes* did that—he also disliked Diderot, and suspected the militant atheism of Holbach and Helvétius as yet another form of intolerance. He disapproved of the radical note in Beaumarchais' *Marriage of Figaro*, and, as has been seen, in the up-and-coming young German pre-romantics. Sense, not sensibility, discipline, not liberation, duty, not freedom were his watchwords, in the conflict of life as on the battlefield. Enlightenment itself was 'a light from heaven for the educated—but a firebrand for the mob'. To the end, in his eyes, the people remained the *canaille*. Rousseau, Diderot, Mirabeau, Lessing and Winckelmann saw him as an out-and-out despot; in Kant's view, his Enlightenment simply boiled down to: 'Reason as much as you like and on any subject you please—but obey'. He sought, says Professor Horn, to make Prussia 'an authoritarian bulwark against the liberal ideas that were slowly gaining ground in western Europe'.

In most respects, as we have seen, his domestic policies were conservative; far more conservative than those of Frederick-William I or the Great Elector. Reason for Frederick was a tool for increasing the power of the State, not for altering the structure of society or genuinely encouraging greater individual freedom and happiness: 'We are not born to be happy, but to do our duty'. The Prussia he bequeathed was the 'well-ordered' State, dominated by drill-sergeants, Junker officers, conscientious bureaucrats and obedient, well-fed citizens.

Professor Holborn argues that Frederick's conservatism was reluctant, forced on him by the inexorable dictates of power politics, pointing out that it 'stands in contrast to his intellectual and religious radicalism'. But in his social outlook, it may be doubted whether Frederick at any stage showed any trace of radicalism, as opposed to paternalism and humanitarianism.

His view of Progress was not optimistic; for while he welcomed scientific, technological and material advance (see his *Discourse on the Utility of the Arts and Sciences*), his view of history did not suggest a view of man in the mass as basically good and capable of virtue, a conclusion confirmed and embittered by experience. In regarding human nature as a constant, and mankind—'that accursed race' ('*cette maudite race*')—as 'savage beasts' 'ruled by passion, and very seldom by reason', however, was his view so very far from that of Voltaire and Gibbon, of history in the main as a 'register of the crimes, follies and misfortunes of mankind'? Man's natural instincts, far from requiring freer development, as Rousseau urged in *Emile*, must be carefully directed into channels that were socially and politically responsible. Frederick's attitude towards himself and his subjects is epitomized in his description of his great land-reclamation schemes—'the triumph of diligence over ignorance and laziness'.

To his deterministic view of man as a 'clockwork machine', there was a partial exception: the 'great man' in history, free from the superstitions and prejudices of the mob, could, by constant supervision, 'tame this beast' and drive it some way forward. But even he should learn to moderate his aims: 'We should not believe that we can shape events; but when they present themselves, we must seize them in order to exploit them'. Compared to the boundless ambition of Napoleon, his aims were modest: 'Man cannot change the nature of things; but I think that by dint of hard work and application one can succeed in improving a barren terrain ... and that is something to be getting on with.' His whole career was the triumph of will-power over daunting adversity—upbringing, war, near defeat, ill-health—but will-power made sane, wholesome and fruitful by the constant exercise of reason and control.

This control he applied to himself as much as to his people. It is evident in his devotion to classical stoicism, his love of Augustanism in literature and the severely disciplined passion of Racine; and in his own self-mastery, the simplicity of his way of life, his complete lack of self-deception or illusions of grandeur. His studied pose of infallibility stemmed from his conviction that it was necessary for the State. His dignity never verged on pomposity, but was tempered by a genuine modesty, occasional delightful sparks of geniality and a saving vein of self-mockery. Towards the end of his life, he said that he owed the public an apology 'for having had the impertinence to live so long, for having bored it and wearied it for three quarters of a century, which is past a joke'. He was a stoic with a sense of humour, an epicurean with a sense of duty. He was too much the sceptic to accept the stoic belief in a guiding providence: the epicurean view of the universe as a meaningless jumble of atoms, of life subject to the imponderable quirks of 'His Sacred Majesty—Chance', seemed closer to observable reality. As to Progress and perfectability—his lips would curl in a bitter smile when he contemplated Prussia's likely fate under his heir-apparent—'that incorrigible creature'. Speculation, however, was fruitless; and meanwhile, as long as he could still draw breath—for his asthma was troublesome—there was work to be done.

When the daily post-load of cabinet orders from Sans-Souci failed to arrive, the people of Berlin knew for certain that Frederick the Great was dead.

Figure 28 Death-mask of Frederick the Great. Photograph from Cambridge University Library.

Chronology

1712	Frederick born, 24 January
1713	Accession of Frederick's father, Frederick-William I
1730	Frederick attempts to flee from Prussia, is imprisoned on his father's orders at Küstrin and compelled to witness the execution of his friend, Katte
1733	Frederick is obliged to marry Elisabeth Christina of Brunswick-Bevern. Retires to his estate at Rheinsberg
1739	Frederick writes his *Anti-Machiavel*
1740	Frederick accedes on death of Frederick-William I. Frederick invades Silesia
1741	Prussian victory over Austrians at Mollwitz
1742	Prussian victory over Austrians at Chotusitz
1745	Prussian victory over Austrians at Hohenfriedberg. Frederick signs Treaty of Dresden with Austria
1746	Frederick begins legal reforms
1747	Palace of Sans-Souci completed
1750–3	Voltaire visits Sans-Souci
1756	Frederick invades Saxony. Seven Years' War begins
1757	Frederick defeats French at Rossbach and Austrians at Leuthen
1758	Frederick 'defeats' Russians at Zorndorf. Death of Frederick's sister Wilhelmine
1759	Prussia defeated by Russians at Kunersdorf
1760	Prussia victorious at Liegnitz and Torgau
1762	Death of Empress Elisabeth of Russia. Russia pulls out of war
1763	Treaty of Hubertusburg terminates Seven Years War. Austria finally renounces Silesia
1764	Frederick concludes alliance with Russia
1772	First Partition of Poland
1778	Prussia fights the War of the Bavarian Succession against Austria
1785	Frederick forms League of German Princes to contain Austrian expansionism
1786	Frederick dies 17 August

Bibliography of Primary Sources

Collected editions of works of Frederick the Great

Fleischauer, C. (ed) 'La réfutation du Prince de Machiavel', *Studies on Voltaire and the Eighteenth Century* Vol 5 (1958), Geneva

Koser, R., Volz, G. B. *et al* (eds) *Politische Correspondenz Friedrichs des Grossen*, 47 vols (1879–1939), Berlin

Preuss, F. D. E. (ed) *Oeuvres de Frédéric le Grand*, 30 vols (1846–56), Berlin

Volz, G. B. (ed) *Die Politischen Testamente Friedrichs des Grossen* (1920), Berlin

Works containing documents by or about Frederick the Great

Besterman, T. (ed) *Voltaire's Correspondence*, 103 vols (1953–64), Geneva

Code Général pour les états prussiens, Vol II (1802), Paris

De Mouy, C. (ed) *Correspondence inédite du roi Stanislas Poniatowski et de Madame Geoffrin* (1875), Paris

De Smitt, F. *Frédéric II, Catherine et le partage de la Pologne, d'après des documents authentiques*, Part II (1861), Paris

Guibert, J. A. H. comte de *Observations on the Military Establishment and Discipline of His Majesty the King of Prussia*, translated from the French by J. Johnson (1780), London

Hubatsch, W. *Frederick the Great of Prussia: Absolutism and Administration* (1975), Thames and Hudson

Koser, R. (ed) *Publicationen aus den Königlichen Preussichen Staatsarchiven*, Vol XXII, *Unterhaltungen mit Friedrich dem Grossen: Memoiren und Tagebücher von Heinrich de Catt* (1884), Leipzig

Latrobe, B. H. (ed) *Characteristic Anecdotes and Miscellaneous Authentic Papers of Frederick II* (1788), London

Lutostanski, K. *Receuil des actes diplomatiques, traités et documents concernant la Pologne*, Vol I *Les partages de la Pologne et la lutte pour l'indépendance* (1918), Paris

Moland, L. (ed) *Oeuvres complètes de Voltaire*, Vol XIX (1879), Paris

Moore, J. *A View of Society and Manners in France, Switzerland and Germany*, Vol II (1789), Dublin

Piggott, F. and Omond, G. W. T. (eds) *Documentary History of the Armed Neutralities 1780 and 1800* (1919), London University Press

Riesbeck, J. C. *Travels through Germany, translated by Mr. Maty*, Vols II and III (1787), London

Stadelmann, R. *Preussens Könige in ihrer Thätigkeit für die Landescultur*, Part II, *Friedrich der Grosse* (1882), Leipzig

von Arneth, A. *Briefe Der Kaiserin Maria Theresia an Ihre Kinder und Freunde*, Vol 1 (1881), Vienna

Recommended Further Reading

Works by Frederick

Frederick's writings should be consulted in the collected editions listed above. The only edition known to me in English is *The Posthumous Works of Frederick II, King of Prussia*, translated by T. Holcraft, thirteen volumes (1789), London. This includes the *Anti-Machiavel*, *Essay on Forms of Government and the Duties of Sovereigns*, the *History of My Own Times* and *History of the Seven Years War*. *Frederick the Great on the Art of War* (1966), Collier-Macmillan, contains some useful documents, translated by J. Luuvas. Richard Aldington has translated a selection from the correspondance with Voltaire in *Letters of Voltaire and Frederick the Great*, the Broadway Library of XVIII Century French literature (1927), London. Selected documents of varying importance by and about Frederick appear in a collection edited by L. Snyder, *Frederick the Great*, in the 'Great Lives Observed' series (1971), Prentice Hall.

Some of Frederick's compositions for flute and his Symphony in D are available on gramophone recordings.

Biography

For a short, straightforward factual account see D. B. Horn, *Frederick the Great and the Rise of Prussia* (1964, 1967), English Universities Press. Nancy Mitford has written a personal biography in her usual lively manner in *Frederick the Great* (1970), Hamish Hamilton, but for a serious discussion, based on Frederick's writings, read G. P. Gooch, *Frederick the Great: the Ruler, the Writer, the Man* (1947), Longman.

The best analysis of Frederick against the Prussian and German background is probably still that of his apologist, the German historian, Gerhard Ritter. First delivered as a series of lectures in 1936, with implicit criticisms of the National Socialist regime, Ritter's book is available in a translation by Peter Paret, *Frederick the Great: an Historical Profile* (1968), University of California Press. Paret has also edited a useful collection of historical essays by various authors in *Frederick the Great: a Profile* (1972), Macmillan.

Another useful collection, edited by T. Barker, is *Frederick the Great and the Making of Prussia* in the 'Problems in European Civilisation' series (1972), Holt, Rinehart and Winston. The celebrated biography of Frederick by Carlyle (1858–65) and Macaulay's essay 'Frederick the Great' (1842), though still fascinating reading, are out of date.

Aspects of Frederick's rule

A very useful (but rather indigestible) study of Frederick's rule, based on archival material, is W. Hubatsch, *Frederick the Great of Prussia: Absolutism and Administration*, translated by P. Doran (1973), Thames and Hudson. W. H. Dorn, 'The Prussian bureaucracy in the eighteenth century', *Political Science Quarterly*, September 1931 to June 1932 (3 articles) remains a masterly piece of historical research, which can be supplemented by a recent study by H. C. Johnson, *Frederick the Great and his Officials* (1975), Yale University Press.

On law reform, see H. Weill, *Frederick the Great and Samuel von Cocceji: a study in the reform of the Prussian judicial administration 1740–55* (1961), State Historical Society of Wisconsin.

On Frederick's mercantilism, see W. O. Henderson, *Studies in the Economic Policy of Frederick the Great* (1963), Frank Cass.

For the army, there is an authoritative introduction in chapter 5, 'The Frederician army', of P. Paret, *Yorck and the Era of Reform* (1966), Princeton University Press.

For a critical analysis of Frederician Prussia and the *Aufklärung* at the end of the reign, see H. Brunschwig, *Enlightenment and Romanticism in Eighteenth-Century Prussia*, translated by F. Jellinek (1974), University of Chicago Press.

E. E. Helm has produced a definitive study of a little-known subject in *Music at the Court of Frederick the Great* (1960), University of Oklahoma Press.

Perhaps the most stimulating introduction to eighteenth-century diplomacy in general is the first chapter of A. Sorel, *L'Europe et la Révolution Française* (1885), available in translation by F. Herrick (1964), Harper Torchbooks. On Frederick's outlook on foreign policy, there is a useful chapter in F. Meinecke, *Machiavellism: the Doctrine of Raison d'Etat and its Place in Modern History*, translated by D. Scott (1957), Routledge and Kegan Paul. For the historical controversy on Frederick's responsibility for the Seven Years War, see Sir Herbert Butterfield, 'The reconstruction of an historical episode: the history of the enquiry into the origins of the Seven Years War', chapter 5 of *Man on His Past* (1955), Cambridge University Press. On Poland, see H. H. Kaplan, *The First Partition of Poland* (1962), Columbia University Press.

A204 The Enlightenment